Growing Up Canadian

CANADA AND ITS YOUTH

COME OF AGE 1960-1980

Clyde Woolman

 FriesenPress

One Printers Way
Altona, MB R0G 0B0
Canada

www.friesenpress.com

ISBN
978-1-03-917949-3 (Hardcover)
978-1-03-917948-6 (Paperback)
978-1-03-917950-9 (eBook)

1. HISTORY, SOCIAL HISTORY

Distributed to the trade by The Ingram Book Company

ACKNOWLEDGEMENTS

Many thanks to those brave souls who read versions of early drafts. There is little resemblance between those nascent efforts and the finished work. The final copy of *Growing Up Canadian* is more focussed in substance and more polished in style due to their suggestions and advice.

Maryanne Mackinnon
Mary Ann McCrea
Don McCririck
Leslie Berends
Dave Brummitt
John Carswell
Roy Londry
Dick Markin
Marlene Neil
Sandi Reis
Tiberio Reis

and especially Dave White who withstood the pain of reading several early drafts.

As always, love and appreciation to my wife and life partner, Ileana.

ABOUT THE AUTHOR

www.clydewoolman.com

Growing Up Canadian is Clyde Woolman's eighth book. As a child, he spent hours reading Hardy Boys novels. As an adult author, his first foray into writing full-length manuscripts was revisiting the mystery and adventure of those first-read books. The result was the publication of two young-adult novels—*Smugglers at the Lighthouse* in 2010 and *Yurek: Edge of Extinction* three years later.

Being a full-time author is possible for only a limited pantheon of mega-selling writers who have a guaranteed readership before their latest book hits the shelves. Most novelists rely on real jobs, and teaching history was the author's first. Principal positions came next; at an elementary, a middle, and three secondary schools. Included in those years was a six-year stint as a Superintendent of Schools (CEO). While educators occasionally lament that, "Nobody's gonna believe the stuff that happens. Someone's gotta write it down," the author decided to do just that—and two humorous novels were the result: *Hepting's Road* (2018) and *Dragons at the Schoolhouse Door* (2020). More direct satirical shots aimed at the bottomless pit of educational jargon came with *Edubabble* in 2018 and *High School Edubabble* in 2020.

Never fully abandoning the earlier interest in history, the author's connection to writing about the recent past was rekindled with a 52,000 word "Corporate History," commissioned by a BC school district. This was the first venture into writing historical non-fiction. It was also the spark to complete *Growing Up Canadian*—a journey to revisit the signposts of an era when the author, his generation, and the country they call home came of age.

Clyde Woolman lives on Vancouver Island and makes frequent junkets to Vancouver and Maui. More information about his books can be found at www.clydewoolman.com

PREFACE

This is a unique tale with a wry style—one that traces a generation and a country coming of age told through a series of short descriptors. Since it aims to be unconventional, why provide a standard preface? Why not do something different?

A section of frequently asked questions (FAQs) has become commonplace in the online world. Supposedly this saves time, and more importantly, money. If most of the common questions can be listed and answered online, paying someone to answer customer queries over the telephone seems redundant and awfully old-fashioned. Since readers will usually have questions about a book, the FAQ format could be useful.

Since this preface is being written prior to publication, the FAQs need to be predicted—more aptly named Likely Asked Questions (LAQs) to which the author can respond. So, in the spirit of quirkiness, the following are the LAQs and the response.

What was the motivation behind writing this book?

This is an excellent question and provides the opportunity to launch into stock responses such as lofty aspirations to tell a story and share it with others. Bringing Canadiana to the forefront of the book-buying public was another noteworthy aim. There was a desire to spark the memory cells of now-elder Canadians; and to inform younger ones that the trials and tribulations that they and the country face today are not specific to their generation.

Admittedly, there is more to this answer than the altruism described above (such as selling books), but it seems a tad tacky to elaborate on the profit motive!

Why are the terms 60–80 era and coming of age used so frequently? Why wasn't the term boomer used instead?

Though appearing to be a tricky two-part question, the two segments are related. Firstly, while the baby boomers were born from 1946 to 1964, there is an unfortunate tendency to equate them with the "Woodstock Generation" of hippies, Yippies, and assorted "long-hairs." Yet the counterculture lasted at best five years, from 1967 to 1972. So-called boomers born in 1963 or 1964 were young children when Woodstock occurred. Boomers born in 1946 or 1947 were in their early twenties and many were busy working full-time jobs. Despite the increasing numbers enrolling in post-secondary institutions, most young people went to work after high school. The 60–80 era is a much more inclusive term that encompasses the full twenty years encompassing the Beat Generation of the early 1960s to the disco and polyester period of the late 1970s. It can also include topics not normally associated with boomer lore—Indigenous issues and business topics to name two.

To assist this wide age-range of readers the entries in each chapter are listed in rough chronological order (and alphabetized as well). An entry about a song from 1962 will read as history to those who became teenagers in the late 1970s. Conversely, a person who came of age in the early 1960s may not even recognize a song or movie from 1979. We tend to categorize our personal histories in chronological order so it seemed to make sense to do so in a book about growing up as a Canadian.

Lastly, most references to the boomer generation have an unfortunate tendency to look back in time. While this nostalgia is certainly an important aspect of *Growing Up Canadian*, it is not the only thrust. Coming of age implies moving on to the next part of life for an individual or the next era for a country. Connection to what was to come in the 1980s and beyond is an important feature of the book.

What was the biggest surprise when researching the book?

Being as influenced by American culture as much as the next person, there was a concern that there would not be enough Canadiana to complete a manuscript of sufficient length. Surprisingly, there were more than enough engaging stories. Canada and Canadians were far more interesting in the 60–80 era than given credit for.

Given the wealth of information and the need to include at least some pertinent American (and English) content, a great deal of material was not included. This will likely lead to questions and criticism from some readers who wonder why this person or that event was not mentioned. There may even be a suggestion that those missing subjects be included in a sequel. This is the equivalent of nirvana to a writer who is always looking at the next project and a *Growing Up Canadian II* is already in draft form.

What was your favourite chapter or entry?

There were no favourite entries or chapters. There were individual stories that brought back vivid memories: the October Crisis outlined in Chapter 3, the musical theatre productions named in Chapter 6 and the Phil Esposito interview referred to in Chapter 7. Some entries were especially interesting since the author had little or no initial knowledge—the Denny of the Mugwamps piece in Chapter 2 and the George Klippert entry in Chapter 3 (A Gay Man Pays a High Price) being two. The origins of McCain Foods, the explosion of Wonderbra sales described in Chapter 6, and the Johnny Bright saga (Bright Days for a Black Athlete) in Chapter 10 also come to mind.

Chapter 4 (Keeping Up with Being Cool) has several entries with a strong personal attachment. Like most young people of the day, the author wanted to appear to be at least somewhat cool (with little success). The Bags for Marbles and Real Booze for an Adult Date entries are two examples that come straight from personal experience. So too was the entry on Seeking Style in the Basement. As for the entry on polyester clothing (Wrinkle-free Duds), a few such shirts covered the body in the late 1970s. A few overseas jaunts included Istanbul, but not Kathmandu (Overland Trail). And while no disco records were purchased, the Bump was attempted at various late 1970s weddings, mercifully without any grinding.

How would you classify Growing Up Canadian?

Hmm, that is a tough question. Though every effort has been made to ensure the information is correct, *Growing Up Canadian* is non-fiction story-telling and nowhere near an academic work (hence the lack of formal references). It is part popular history, part satirical humour, part pop-culture, part social commentary; and possibly a few other parts as well. In this sense, the book defies a pure classification. In the end, the real test of any book is whether the reader enjoys it. If so, even though there is a tendency to group many aspects of contemporary life into "niche demographics" or "identity politics," classifying this work as an example of one particular genre of writing or another seems irrelevant.

CONTENTS

1

AN ELECTRONIC HEARTH FOR

THE MODERN HOME

In the mid-1950s the television set began to assume pride-of-place in Canadian homes. By 1960 it was a new type of central hearth. This electronic model sent the once-showpiece fireplace to the back burner. It arrived as a miniscule screen showing a grainy black and white image that was buried in a boxy cabinet. Lucky families living near the American border could get more TV stations than that provided by the Canadian Broadcasting Corporation (CBC). The youngest sibling could be made useful by standing beside the set and gripping the rabbit ears for better reception. However, the technology changed rapidly. In just over a scant ten years the screens became much larger and sales of the new colour TVs would match and then soon overtake black-and-white models.

In the 60–80 period Canadian television producers became adept at specific types of TV shows—news, journalism, sports (particularly hockey), and political and social satire. These strengths have continued to this day. Success in producing other types of programming such as variety shows, sitcoms, and dramas remained elusive in the 60–80 era with only a few notable exceptions. By the late 1960s more and more American TV programs were flooding into Canada since the airwaves cared little for national boundaries. The rabbit ears eventually disappeared as the American onslaught arrived, initially via unsightly antennas perched on suburban rooftops. Later it was through the even more border-busting introduction of cablevision.

AN AMERICAN GIANT BEFRIENDS THE KIDS

The Friendly Giant was an American. At least originally. Bob Homme, who played the giant for the entire TV run from 1954 to 1985, was born in Wisconsin. He became a Canadian citizen in the early 1990s after the program had ended. The TV version of the show (it had been on radio for one year) began in 1954 in his home state before moving to National Education Television in the U.S. In one of the few examples of the CBC picking up an American program and making it its own, production of *The Friendly Giant* moved to Toronto in 1958. It remained there until the show was cancelled, 27 years later.

"Look up. Look w-a-a-a-y up." This opening segment enabled the children at home to get a better look at the big guy. The gentle-voiced giant would let the drawbridge down and open the front doors. One or two miniature chairs were set in place. He would invite his pals, Rusty the Rooster and Jerome the Giraffe, for a nice quiet chat and perhaps a song or two. There was no jolt of anarchic action on this show. The never-changing set was inexpensive. The music was calm and soothing; the dialogue was soft, the vibe gentle. The entire aura was low-key to the point of somnambulance. Yet the fifteen minutes seemed to fly by. The Friendly Giant would play his recorder. The chairs were put away. The drawbridge was pulled up. The doors closed on another session as the children were invited to visit again.

The children did. Again, and again—and their children did too.

A WISE-CRACKING TURTLE

The "Tiger Rag" was written in 1917 and a sped-up version was used to open the CBC TV show, *Razzle Dazzle*. This helped create the fast-paced and chaotic vibe that was the cornerstone of the show. The program was an after-school must-see for thousands of Canadian children from 1961 to 1966. It was initially hosted by Michelle Finney and Alan Hamel, the latter entertainer later marrying Suzanne Somers and hosting *The Alan Hamel Show* on CTV in the late 1970s.

The humans may have received top billing on the credits for *Razzle Dazzle*, but Howard the Turtle was the breakout comedic star. He told horrible jokes known as groaners. One example was, "I have 10,000 bones in my body. Do you know why? I had sardines for lunch." Howard was a skilled impresario. With a flip of headwear he could alter character. A few of his common roles were Howard Mellotone, a pop star; Jimmy Fiddle Faddle, a Hollywood gossip columnist; and Howard Threadneedle, a poet. The turtle received thousands of hand-written letters from child viewers and is currently resting on his laurels in the Canadian Museum of History.

Razzle Dazzle welcomed audience participation. Children could write in and join the Razzle Dazzle Fan Club. They could also send for a secret decoder wheel which could be used to decipher secret messages that would appear on the screen during future episodes. Since Canada was actively engaged in the Cold War against the dastardly Soviets, it was never too early to start training children in the art of spying and subterfuge.

BEN CARTWRIGHT – LADIES' MAN

Ottawa-born and one-time CBC radio broadcaster Lorne Greene landed the lead role of Ben Cartwright in the long running (1959–1973) TV series Bonanza. In a stunning lack of foresight, the CBC did not pick up the series until 1961.

Greene played Ben Cartwright, the perfect father figure, wise and patient yet tough when he needed to be. The character was widowed three times with each wife birthing one of his three boys. This explained why Adam, Hoss, and Little Joe had only a passing resemblance as brothers. Adam's mother, Elizabeth, was English. A Swedish woman, Inger, was the mother of Hoss. To keep the varied ancestry going (Ben was clearly a worldly man when it came to love), Marie was Little Joe's mother. She was of French Creole ethnicity.

After three marriages, Ben's sex drive was showing signs of petering out— but his boys were eager to pick up the slack. Unfortunately, they did not have much luck with women as they always seemed to strike out on the romance front. In many episodes, when amorous sparks landed on the Cartwright sons they were doused by the woman's illness, an accident, or other unfortunate circumstance.

When Greene finally hung up his spurs in 1973 (the CBC cancelled *Bonanza* in 1970), he landed another starring role in a TV series with *Battlestar Galactica* in 1978. The Canadian once again played a wise father-figure. However, he did not seem to take to space travel the same way he did to horses and wagons. The first Galactica series was cancelled after one season. There was no word on whether any of the Battlestar characters had been the result of any intergalactic coitus—*see Chapter 2, Making a One-Hit Wonder (2)*.

CANADA'S GOOD, BAD, AND UGLY

A young person in the 1960s did not need to go to Sunday school or read a fable to be introduced to the difference between right and wrong; good and evil. It was there every week on TV in the form of professional wrestling. Unlike the bulked-up male and female beefcake of today who perform stunts that are clearly choreographed, the 1960s wrestlers who staged their shows in the main wrestling hubs of Ontario and Québec were usually overweight, unathletic, and flabby. Somehow this made them seem more human—more real; especially on a flickering black and white screen. There are many wrestlers who could be mentioned in this entry but only four have been included. They represent a classic tag-team match between the good and bad guys.

Whipper Billy Watson had a reputation for clean wrestling, befitting due to his Toronto-area upbringing. While this made him vulnerable to the rule-breaking bad guys, Whipper still did well, defeating the likes of Gorgeous George and Lou Thesz before large audiences at Maple Leaf Gardens.

Despite his moniker, Yukon Eric was an American, the only one in this foursome. Not being especially strong in geography, Yukon Eric was usually advertised as being from Fairbanks, Alaska. He portrayed a good guy by wrestling cleanly and obeying the rules while wearing his checkered lumberjack shirt.

Killer Kowlaski hailed from Windsor, Ontario. He was a villain and a pretty good one at that. In a real ring mishap he knocked off Yukon Eric's ear. Ever the bad guy, he showed little remorse when he visited the stricken man in the hospital. Despite his villainy, Killer Kowalski displayed a soft side, billing himself as wrestling's only vegetarian. This may explain why he did not chew on Yukon Eric's ear.

Gene Kiniski did not need a special name like "Killer" or "Whipper." Instead, he billed himself as "Canada's greatest athlete." Born in Edmonton, he had played for the then-named Edmonton Eskimos so he could at least claim participation in two professional athletic endeavours. Prior to relocating to Vancouver, Kiniski had some storied feuds with Whipper Billy Watson and Yukon Eric, thus cementing his loutish bad guy image.

CANINE HOBO

The first incarnation of *The Littlest Hobo* (La Vagabond, en francais) TV show was produced from 1963 to 1965. Unlike its successor which began in 1979, the original version was in black and white. It was shown in syndication and shot in British Columbia. The title was apropos. In the North American vernacular of the day a tramp was a person who travelled but avoided work. A hobo was a person who travelled and was willing to work. The German Shepherd star did not shirk responsibility. A program entitled The Littlest Tramp would not have accurately reflected the show's overarching theme.

So, what work did the canine hobo engage in, aside from being a stalwart actor? In episode upon episode the dog would arrive and provide needed assistance to an often-hapless human or two. Despite being loved and wanted it would wander away, seemingly happy to rid itself of the burden of caring for the two-legged creatures. The program was not blessed with a big budget. The sets were sparse, the camera angles limited, and the sound tinny. On more than one occasion the canine was the best actor.

CAN WE SEE THAT AGAIN?

It would seem impossible to watch televised sports in the 1960s and beyond without instant replay. No longer was there danger in missing important action while grabbing a beer from the fridge or digging out the potato chips from a cupboard. There was always a second or third look at what had happened.

Video replay was a Canadian invention. The first time the technology was tried was on *Hockey Night in Canada* during a telecast of a Toronto Maple Leaf game in 1955. The technology was not yet videotape (that was to come one year later) so the initial year's attempts meant there was "near-instant" replay that could be viewed by the audience about 30 seconds later.

By 1963 the technology had improved, but it was still tough to get an instant video replay machine into the sportscaster's booth since it weighed 1,300 pounds. By the late 1960s the technology had improved and a match was made in heaven between video replay and televised football.

Video replay is most effective when there is action followed by a lull so the video could be replayed and analyzed. The technology was only a moderately-good fit for baseball since there is often a lot more lull than action. Few in the TV audience can get emotionally charged when watching video replays of a batter whiffing on a pitch, a routine grounder hit to the shortstop, or the fourth lame attempt by a pitcher to pick off a runner at first base.

However, football was perfect. Intense short-duration action was followed by a long lull as players huddled together to chat about what to do next. Cameras could be linked to a separate videotape machine that could highlight individual players and what they did or did not do on the previous play. Slow motion accentuated the crushing tackles, a dropped pass, or a less-than-fortuitous fumble. Legitimized violence and player errors combined to provide a totally new perspective on the game. This made football much more entertaining for the home fan and drew much larger audiences. This meant more advertising. This meant bigger TV contracts. This meant … well, the result seems obvious.

EVEN A MOUNTIE HAS NEEDS

Cartoon characters Boris Badenov and Natasha Fatale were portrayed as diabolical yet bumbling Russian spies on *The Adventures of Rocky and Bullwinkle* throughout the 1960s. As a separate segment, the lone "Canadian" on the program made his debut in 1961 and was a fixture for much of the decade. Dudley Do-Right of the Mounties was honest and conscientious though not blessed with a big brain. He was not very creative either, apparently failing to come up with a name for his horse other than—Horse.

Despite his intellectual and creative shortcomings, Dudley the Mountie was featured in other syndicated cartoons and even received top billing in a short-lived animated show beginning in 1969.

Doing things right resulted in Dudley eventually besting his nemesis, Snidely Whiplash. This was usually the result of sheer dumb luck rather than any investigative prowess. Yet the Canadian justice system is forever lenient. Snidely always seemed to be avoid long periods of incarceration and would reappear in the next episode to cause various forms of villainous mayhem.

Nell Fenwick was the daughter of the Mounties' boss and thus a target for the dastardly Snidely. Dudley would constantly save Nell, the classic damsel in distress. As clueless as her red-tunic-wearing saviour, Nell would be dim-witted enough to fall into another of Snidely's traps in the next episode. Her apparent less-than-average intelligence may have explained the failure to notice Dudley's obvious feelings for her. She seemed more taken with Dudley's horse. Being shunned in favour of his equine pal did not seem to douse Dudley's infatuation with the lovely Nell. However, try as he might to impress young Nell, she always displayed more interest in his horse.

GHOULISH CANADIAN MUNSTER

If there was an iron law of American television in the early-mid-1960s it was, "If it works do it again—and again—and again." In the time that one could say "poof," sitcoms featuring magic and fantasy popped up like bubbles in a champagne glass. There were shows starring a talking horse (*Mr. Ed*), a spaceman (*My Favorite Martian*), ghouls (*Addams Family*), genies (*I Dream of Jeannie*), campy superheroes (*Batman*), witches (*Bewitched*), and the most ridiculous of all, a car (*My Mother the Car*).

Into this mix stepped Margaret Yvonne Middleton, born and raised in Vancouver. After graduating from high school in the BC city, Miss Middleton's mother whisked her away to Los Angeles in search of stardom. The young woman found it as Yvonne De Carlo. She often portrayed exotic women in biblical films, including playing Moses' mother in the epic, *The Ten Commandments*. When the demand for those types of roles dissipated, De Carlo was no longer on the Hollywood "A list." Looking for work, she was cast as mother Lily in the TV show, *The Munsters*. Vampire Lily had to deal with her clumsy Frankenstein-like husband Herman, eccentric Grandpa, the precocious son Eddie, and the attractive and therefore abnormal daughter, Marilyn. When she was asked how she was to play a ghoulish mother, De Carlo stated, "I followed the directions I was given ... play her like Donna Reed."

At the time there were only three major American networks and shows were scheduled against each other to compete in certain timeslots. After only two seasons, *The Munsters* was cancelled in 1966 after getting clobbered in its time-slot by *Batman*.

JUSTICE – RAYMOND BURR STYLE

"We couldn't afford a big star." So said the executive producer of the upcoming TV show *Perry Mason* in 1957. Enter burly Raymond Burr, born in New Westminster, BC. Although he spent most of his childhood years in the United States, the *New York Times* reported that as a 12-year-old he had his first acting work in Vancouver. When casting began for *Perry Mason*, Burr was working steadily as an actor, though he was not yet a household name.

Burr first read for the character of perennially losing attorney Hamilton Burger. He impressed the decision makers and was told to lose weight before the next round of auditions. Burr did so and he and 50 others read for the Mason part. So did William Hopper who was chosen to play private detective, Paul Drake. Burr's Mason lost only two cases during the 1957 to 1966 run. Rival attorney Hamilton Burger was adept at regularly snatching defeat from the jaws of victory. Mason had a winning record that would have been the envy of the Montreal Canadiens of the late 1970s. This must have allowed him to charge his clients exorbitant fees. That would explain how he was able to keep the chain-smoking Mr. Drake fully employed and have a full-time secretary, Della Street, who was rarely seen anywhere near a typewriter.

Burr did not lose a beat after the Mason series, starring in *Ironside* from 1967 to 1975. Shot and paralyzed from the waist down, Burr's Ironside character was driven around in a specially equipped van by former street-thug-turned-good, Mark Sanger. Justice was once again served. Without fail Ironside used his brains to apprehend the bad guys.

Burr passed away in California in 1993 and was interred alongside his parents at a cemetery in New Westminster, BC.

KIRK CHEWS THE SCENERY

Though he has had a long and varied acting career that began at the Stratford Festival in Ontario, Montreal native William Shatner is best known in the 60–80 period for his 1960s role as Captain Kirk in the TV show, *Star Trek*. The show was almost cancelled during the first season due to low ratings. It was saved by the new network policies that involved diving deeper into the audience demographics—*who* watched the program mattered as much as how many tuned in. It was the nascent years of niche demographics in TV decision-making. *Star Trek* appealed to the younger demographic much coveted by advertisers. The program stayed on the air for three years. At the time no one would have believed that with its Styrofoam boulders and budget-conscious, almost comedic special effects, the show would become a cult classic and spawn an entire industry of merchandise, future TV shows, and movies.

Central to all this was William Shatner. He overacted the Kirk character to such an extent that his fellow actors watched with chagrin as he grabbed the stage and chewed the scenery. His on-camera swagger, pregnant pauses in speech, and ability to writhe in excruciating agony created a field day for a generation of 1970s stand-up comics mimicking his style.

There was usually one question hanging in the balance when Shatner's overacting is the topic—was it truly bad acting or the effect a product of a skilled thespian?

MISS KITTY'S PROFESSION

The Canadian fascination with American TV westerns appeared to fade in the 1970s. Why they were so popular in the late 1950s and early 1960s with shows such as *Rawhide, Wagon Train, Have Gun Will Travel, Maverick, et al* is a mystery. Perhaps an easily understood tale of good versus evil transcends any nationalist sentiment.

Of the dozens of westerns beaming across the border, *Gunsmoke* was one of the most popular and long-lasting, airing in Canada from 1960 to 1975. Unlike many of its ilk, the show had a permanent female character. Amanda Blake played Miss Kitty, the owner of the Dodge City saloon and the only female lead for the duration of the show. She appeared in over 500 of the 635 TV episodes, running a saloon which conveniently had rooms upstairs. For some reason dedicated lawman Matt Dillon turned a blind eye to the obvious enterprise Miss Kitty was running on the side. Presumably Dillon was too busy dealing with horse-thieves, bandits, cattle rustlers, and other assorted frontier riff-raff who seemed to populate the territory in and around the town. Despite being the sole female who hung around Dodge City for any length of time, she and Matt never seemed to get to "know" each other, at least in the biblical sense.

The creator of the show, Norman Macdonnell, explained the relationship between Matt and Miss Kitty to *Time* in the 1950s. "Kitty is just someone Matt has to visit every once in a while. She's obviously not selling chocolate bars."

MISTER DRESSUP'S BOTTOMLESS WARDROBE

The clothes make the man. The cliché may be somewhat of an exaggeration. But not in the case of American-born Ernie Coombs who found a home in Canada as Mr. Dressup.

Coombs accompanied fellow American Fred Rogers to Canada after Mr. Rogers had been offered a contract by the CBC. After a few years Mr. Rogers returned to the United States. Coombs meanwhile, had played the Dressup character for three years on CBC's *Butternut Square*. When that program was cancelled, he got top billing on his own show and began the long run as Mr. Dressup. The show started in 1967, one year before Mr. Rogers' started his neighbourhood show south of the border.

Mr. Dressup liked his red steamer trunk which had pride of place in the living room. Even though he never seemed to travel anywhere, the trunk was full of interesting clothes. The most common storyline was Mr. Dressup opening the "tickle trunk" and hauling out a costume which he donned and climbed into character. Usually the episode would involve Mr. Dressup, now in character, yakking with his puppet pals, the child Casey and the dog Finnegan. They resided in a tree house in Dressup's back yard. Why they were never invited to live with the supposedly kindly man in the larger, warmer house is a good question from a logical adult perspective. But tree-house living was a normal state-of-affairs for the children watching the show.

Mr. Dressup found enough costumes for the program to last until the mid-1990s, thus entertaining the children of the children who had first watched the show. It survived the introduction of *Sesame Street* to Canada in 1969 and even beat it in the ratings on occasion.

NUMBING THE MIND FOR THE BOOB TUBE

To a certain degree most fiction, and particularly fantasy and mysticism, requires the suspension of disbelief. Samuel Taylor Coleridge coined the term in the early 1800s. This is not surprising given that a few of his lengthy poems such as *The Rime of the Ancient Mariner* and *Kubla Khan* had strong mystical elements.

It could be argued that many American TV shows popular in Canada in the mid to late 1960s stretched the suspension of disbelief by forcing viewers to ignore any semblance of rational thinking. Perhaps that explains why television had earned the nickname, "the boob tube." The examples of the need to suspend disbelief are numerous and only a few have been included here for the sake of brevity.

The castaways on *Gilligan's Island* could never manage to escape, yet visitors continually dropped in for an episode and then easily departed. In *Hogan's Heroes,* Hogan and his prisoner buddies regularly left *Stalag* 13. They wandered about in the local German region drinking beer and blowing up bridges, even though they could not speak a word of the language. On *Batman,* Commissioner Gordon must have relied on nepotism to become the top dog of Gotham City's police department. That is the only explanation given his complete ineptitude as a detective. Totally clueless, he failed to notice that Batman and Robin's voices sounded pretty much the same as their alter-egos, philanthropist Bruce Wayne and his ward, Dick Grayson.

There was no point in asking logical questions. Just suspend the disbelief and enjoy the show.

TRAINEES ON *THE BEACHCOMBERS*

It was set on the rugged west coast of British Columbia and infused with multi-cultural characters. They displayed respect for the natural landscape and provided a family-oriented mix of comedy and drama—what was not to like about the CBC show, *The Beachcombers*? Not much given its longevity. The show started in 1972 and ran for 18 seasons. In 1998 it was named the most popular CBC series of all time.

Yet critics were never far away, particularly when firing darts at Canadian TV shows. The *Toronto Star* called it, "A typically mind-numbing Canadian TV series ... that inexplicably ran for nearly two decades." CBC Radio host Grant Lawrence said, "It was like the *Dukes of Hazard* on water." The *Canadian Encyclopedia* quoted an academic who stated, "It was, fashionable amongst critics to ignore or denigrate the series." Their panning of a series so popular with viewers is a good example of how out of touch critics can be.

The show was filmed on location in Gibsons BC, a small community north of Vancouver via ferry. The ocean-going scenes were filmed from a custom-built barge that housed cameras, props, costumes, and changerooms. The flexibility that came from shooting scenes from the barge made the quality of production higher than what was normally seen on Canadian programs of the time. It demonstrated that the CBC could produce a half-hour comedy-drama series that did not look or sound much different than American shows. Over the years *The Beachcombers* aired in 50 countries, including Ireland, South Africa, Ukraine, and the then-named communist bastion, East Germany.

It was this development of production values where *The Beachcombers* likely had the most lasting impact. Until that time, most CBC TV pro-duction was centred in Toronto. BC had virtually no film industry. Many working on *The Beachcombers* received a crash course of on-the-job training; they would eventually become the core of a Vancouver-based industry that was later known as "Hollywood North."

WAXMAN ON THE KING'S THRONE

In the early 1970s the American sitcom world was turned on its head. Gone were the fantasy shows like *My Favourite Martian, I Dream of Jeannie*, and *The Munsters*. Gone too were programs that featured honest but naïve rural rubes featured in *The Beverly Hillbillies, Green Acres*, and *Petticoat Junction*. The new-era sitcom focussed on "real" folks, facing "real" issues. Shows such as *All in the Family, Mary Tyler Moore, MASH, Sanford and Son, Maude*, and *One Day at a Time* hit the airwaves.

The CBC tried its hand at a sitcom that followed the general American trend. In came *The King of Kensington* which had a very successful run from 1975 to 1980. Toronto native Al Waxman played an owner of a convenience store who was the local "king" of an urbanized, multicultural community. He spent his time yakking with an ethnic menagerie of buddies about life and politics while resolving disputes and minor conflicts with Solomon-like common sense.

Some critics thought the show was too close a facsimile to *All in the Family*. Yet Waxman's character leaned liberal and his mother was the conservative right-wing foil, a reversal of the Archie-Michael relationship on the American program. Both shows did break barriers. They brimmed with political humour. They broke new ground, the American show by featuring an annoying bigot—the Canadian one by reflecting a multi-ethnic Toronto neighbourhood, an aspect of the cultural mosaic that had not been previously portrayed on Canadian TV.

After *The King of Kensington* ended, Waxman landed the role of a police supervisor in the 1980s American police drama *Cagney and Lacey;* a long-running (7 years) TV buddy show that broke different barriers by featuring two female police officers.

2

BEGINNINGS OF A POP MUSIC PARADE

It would be nice to say that those coming of age in the 60–80 era enjoyed a distinct Canadian sound. It would be nice to say that many Canadian artists were international sensations. It would be nice to say, except it was not true. The only two notable exceptions were jazz pianist Oscar Peterson ("the man with four hands") and classical pianist Glenn Gould, "one of the most acclaimed musicians of the twentieth century." Though they may be considered from an earlier era, both pianists won multiple Grammy Awards in the 1970s and later.

However, folk, pop, and rock music was the soul food of the generation that came of age in the 60–80 era. And it was English and American musicians in the kitchen. This was an era when only a handful of Canadian artists such as Paul Anka, Neil Young, Joni Mitchell, and Anne Murray reached ongoing cross-border appeal. Despite this, the foundation was being laid for an explosion of Canadian success on the pop-rock international stage in the decades to come. The next generation or two would include the likes of Bryan Adams, Shania Twain, Alanis Morissette, Avril Lavigne, Celine Dion, Justin Bieber, and Drake, amongst others.

AL AND THE SILVERTONES

This Winnipeg-based group later became known as Chad Allan and the Reflections. It later morphed into Chad Allan and the Expressions. Just as the band's popularity began to rise, leader Allan left. In the quick-rise world of pop music, timing is everything.

In 1965 the group recorded a cover version of "Shakin' All Over," originally a hit in the U.K. for Johnny Kidd and the Pirates. The Chad Allan version topped the charts in Canada and hit #22 in the U.S. (* except where noted all rankings reflect the U.S. Billboard Hot 100). Unable to choose a better band name and wishing to hide the group's origins in the music hinterland called Canada, a promotional gimmick was hatched. With the Guess Who? as the band's name on the label fans were left wondering who the group really was. Many young listeners would logically believe it to be part of the invasion of English bands, perhaps even a famous one!

Chad Allan left the Guess Who shortly thereafter to be replaced by lead vocalist, Burton Cummings. (Later, Allan joined the band Brave Belt with Randy Bachman, but once again left before major success, this time with Bachman-Turner Overdrive). The Guess Who teaser name seemed to be as good as any so the moniker was retained. With a gig on a less-than-memorable Canadian TV show called *Let's Go*, the band was becoming known across Canada. Recognition in the U.S. took longer. Their breakthrough 1969 hit "These Eyes" reached the top ten, eventually peaking at #6 (#7 in Canada). Pop/rock aficionados in the United States no longer had to guess who the band was—*see Chapter 10, Oh! It Was About American Girls!*

ANKA GROWS UP

The poster child for the teen heartthrob brigade of the late 1950s and early 1960s was Ottawa-born Paul Anka. He topped the charts with hit songs in Canada and the U.S. such as "Diana," "Lonely Boy," and "Puppy Love" in 1958, 1959, and 1960. He wrote the latter song for Annette Funicello of *Mickey Mouse Club* fame with whom he had an infatuation—along with most other young males of the day.

Anka was a strong songwriter. Even when his stage-style was swamped by the Beatles and others in the English musical invasion of the mid to late 1960s, he continued with success. Early in his career he had penned "It Doesn't Matter Anymore" for Buddy Holly, ironic given the tragedy that would befall Holly shortly afterward. For much of the 1960s and early 1970s

Anka's song-writing reflected a middle-aged sensibility. There was little point in him attempting to write songs for The Rolling Stones or Led Zeppelin. Instead, his hits came from the voices of artists such as Tom Jones ("She's A Lady") and Frank Sinatra ("My Way").

Along with fellow early 1960s chart-topper Neil Sedaka, Anka burst back onto the recording scene in the mid-1970s with the #1 hit "You're Having My Baby" in 1974. "One Man Woman" followed and reached #7 in 1975. "I Don't Like to Sleep Alone" was another top ten single that year (#8). Though these three hits were steeped in sexual connotation, there was little likelihood that the now more mature middle-aged Anka was singing them to former dream-girl Funicello.

CANADA'S "ALL-INDIAN" BAND

When a group was billed as Canada's All-Indian Band, the last gig anyone would expect to see them perform would be the second Inaugural Ball for U.S. President Richard Nixon in 1973. But that is where the Washington D.C. political elite saw Billy ThunderKloud and the Chieftones. Given that the country-music band was playing at state fairs at the time, it was likely to be the only occasion when the Washington power brokers would catch the act. Why the band received the invitation is a mystery.

The answer may be linked to two major themes for that evening. Firstly, it was important that the event break even financially. The cost to hire the Chieftones was considerably less than bringing in Frank Sinatra. Secondly, the food featured a broad selection of cuisine from minority and ethnic groups that made up the American social fabric. Perhaps the "all-Indian" Chieftones were a suitable complement to the table offerings. Since the band was based in the U.S. by that time, the fact that they were Canadian must have been lost on the organizers.

The leader of the group was Vincent Clifford who was a member of the *Gitsan* band of the *Tsimshian* nation of northwestern BC. When an early teen, Vincent left to attend the St. Albert Residential School in Edmonton where he met a heretofore unknown brother, Barry. Three other Indigenous boys joined the brothers and formed the band known as the Chieftones. They showcased their country sound in the area before moving to Toronto and later to the U.S. Albert Canadien was an original band member of Dene heritage. He left the group in 1969 and eventually became the Director of Official Languages for the Northwest Territories.

When Vincent changed his name to the more Indigenous-sounding Billy ThunderKloud, the other members followed with the monikers, Jack Wolf, Richard Grayowl, and Barry Littlestar. Publicity photos featured the members in feathered headdress and other Indigenous-inspired clothing and regalia. With a 1974 Nashville recording contract in hand the group broke onto the country charts in the mid to late 1970s. The most commercially successful release was "What Time of Day?" in 1975 which reached #16 on the Billboard Hot Country charts. ThunderKloud was chosen as the Outstanding Indian (the term at the time) of the Year by the American Indian Exposition in that same year. He and the band continued to tour well into the 1980s.

CONNECTION POINT FOR STILLS AND YOUNG

It was 1970 when the towns of Port Arthur, Fort William, and the surrounding areas amalgamated to form Thunder Bay, Ontario. Fort William sat 552 kilometres northeast of Minneapolis and 701 kilometres east of Winnipeg. From a North American music industry perspective the town perched on the edge of the Canadian Shield was in the proverbial middle of nowhere.

Yet it was here that two of the best-known musicians of the 60–80 era first met in 1965. Stephen Stills (who would later be unsuccessful in his audition for the *Monkees* TV show) was with his band, The Company. Touring through small Fort William at the Canadian head of Lake Superior was a good indication that Stills had not yet reached international stardom.

The back-up band that night was the Canadian group The Squires, led by Neil Young. The members were from Winnipeg and had settled in Fort William for a time to make a record or two in the Canadian wilderness. This indicated that Mr. Young was hardly in line to appear on *The Ed Sullivan Show*.

Stills and Young met that night and became friends. Young moved to the United States and he and Stills played together in the band Buffalo Springfield, which did appear on Sullivan's popular Sunday night program.

Later, the group Crosby, Stills, Nash, and Young did not. They found an even better gig than the Sullivan show—the 1969 Woodstock festival.

In the 1970s Young and Stills had successful solo careers that included flitting in and out of various bands. Young's most successful commercial release at the time was *Harvest* which was the best-selling album in the U.S. in 1972. "Heart of Gold" was the most popular single from the album and remains Young's only #1 hit.

DENNY OF THE MUGWAMPS

Halifax native Denny Doherty was a member of the pop group, The Mugwamps. Never heard of them? That is understandable since the band was together for one year (1964) and their one album and two singles were released after they had disbanded. What is notable is that one of Doherty's bandmates was Cass Elliot. He and Elliot later joined with John and Michelle Phillips to form The Mamas and the Papas. The other two Mugwamps members did not do too badly either. Fellow Canadian Zal Yanovsky and American John Sebastian would eventually help form another very successful group—the Lovin' Spoonful. Doherty sang lead on the song "California Dreamin'," one of the Mamas and Papas' biggest hits. It reached #3 in Canada in early 1966 (#4 in the U.S.).

Internal relationships were often a minefield in 1960s pop groups. Keeping all the youthful members of a suddenly famous group paddling the canoe in the same direction through the swirling rapids of the recording industry was tough work. When a band had an even split of male and female members (very unusual at the time) and one duo was married, there was a good chance someone was going to throw the paddles overboard and the canoe was going to spend some time thrashing about in turbulent water.

Prior to the big hits of 1966 Doherty was having an affair with fellow group member Michelle Phillips. Her co-band husband John was not impressed, though he and Doherty were able to eventually reconcile. Cass Elliot was not impressed either—and stayed that way. She had a romantic interest in Doherty that was not reciprocated. In a 2007 *Vanity Fair* article Michelle Phillips claimed Cass Elliot told her, "I don't get it. You could have any man you want. Why did you take mine?" (Doherty). It would not be a stretch to think a little sexual promiscuity added to the "artistic differences" which led to the group's split in 1968 (Michelle Phillips had been briefly fired from the group due to a relationship with a member of The Byrds).

Michelle and John Phillips divorced in 1969. She went on to a successful acting career, including a regular role on the evening soap opera *Knot's Landing* in the early 1990s. In those same years John Phillips struggled with drug and alcohol issues. Doherty returned to Halifax and played the Harbour Master on the children's TV show *Theodore Tugboat* from 1993 to 2001. He passed away in 2007.

ED'S IMPORT BUSINESS

Canadians coming of age in the 1960s could always check out the latest in music by watching *The Ed Sullivan Show* on Sunday night. Sullivan always had, as he put it, "something for the youngsters." In the early 1960s he showcased Canadians Paul Anka and Robert Goulet, though the latter was hardly appealing to the youth market. In the mid-1960s the Guess Who made an appearance. By the late 1960s several groups with at least a Canadian presence: Buffalo Springfield, The Band, and Steppenwolf graced the Sunday-night screen.

There were Motown acts with their smooth dance moves and spiffy costumes for men and women—The Supremes, Smokey Robinson and the Miracles, and Gladys Knight and the Pips amongst others. Somehow the Motown crews always looked more debonair than the white-skinned acts who never seemed to be able to match the sartorial splendour. Many other groups, such as The Young Rascals, Paul Revere and the Raiders, the Turtles, the Beach Boys, and the very surly, very sexy, Jim Morrison leading The Doors, crossed the Sullivan stage.

But the really cool pop/rock acts that appeared on the show spoke English with a funny accent as a hurricane of English bands blew over the Atlantic Ocean and stormed the stage. For U.K. performers, an invite to be on *Ed Sullivan* was like stepping through the front door of the magical palace that was the American market.

Of course, the Beatles were the first of the English bands to be featured. On February 9, 1964, an estimated 73 million Americans tuned in. Given that Canada had approximately one-tenth the U.S. population it is logical to add another seven million to that total. Soon after, the stampede was on. The Dave Clark Five appeared on the show 18 times. Other English acts were not far behind in the parade across Sullivan's stage; the Rolling Stones, the Animals, the Hollies, Lulu, The Zombies, Herman's Hermits, Petula Clark, Gerry and the Pacemakers, Cilla Black, The Moody Blues, The Who, and more.

Each act had a record or two that was either being introduced to, or sold in, the North American market. Appearing on *Ed Sullivan* made for a guaranteed audience and exposure that was far better than any purchased advertising. The wily Mr. Sullivan had a foothold on a seemingly bottomless pit of English talent geared to the young demographic. Outsourcing his product in the form of young entertainers, Ed's import business had no need for cargo ships, port facilities, or retail outlets. As the tide of English bands slowed, Sullivan's show lost steam and it was cancelled in 1971. He passed away three years later.

MCCARTNEY'S ONTARIO BADGE

One of the most iconic images of the 1960s is the cover of the 1967 Beatles' album, *Sgt. Pepper's Lonely Hearts Club Band*. Dressed in semi-military, semi-showband uniforms, the Beatles stand in front of their own grave. Behind them are the faces of dozens of famous personalities ranging from Mae West to Edgar Allan Poe, Carl Jung to Fred Astaire, and Karl Marx to Bob Dylan. A careful look at the back-cover photo of Paul McCartney's blue uniform reveals an Ontario Provincial Police insignia (OPP) on his upper left arm. Explanations of how McCartney came in possession of the badge vary.

One version, reported by CTV in 2017 on the 50th anniversary of the album's release, focussed on Sgt. Randall Pepper of the Ontario Police Department (OPP). He ran the security detail for the Beatles when they were briefly in Toronto in 1966. Initially, Mr. Pepper was not a big fan of the Beatles, believing them to be hooligans. This was according to his granddaughter who added, "For whatever reason he was charmed by the Beatles and they were charmed by him." One of Pepper's officers gave four OPP badges to the group. Only McCartney wore it on the uniform photo that graced the back jacket of the album.

It was not the first time McCartney was the outlier (as an example, in the photo gracing the cover of *Abbey Road* he is barefoot, wielding a cigarette, and out of step with the other three Beatles). There were several other examples displaying Paul's uniqueness. For a time, there were many who became ensnared in the hysteria surrounding the Paul-is-dead hints dropped by the band over the years, including the OPP badge. The rabid believers in what was eventually regarded as one of the best publicity stunts of all time, had misread the partially concealed insignia on McCartney's uniform to read OPD, Officially Pronounced Dead.

MAKING A ONE-HIT WONDER

Determining the criteria for a Canadian one-hit wonder is not as easy as it seems. A song may receive considerable airplay in Canada owing to Canadian content rules but not garner much notice in the United States. Nevertheless, the following list of hits were notable in their rocket-like rise to glory before running out of fuel for a second launch.

1. The Beau-Marks (a take on the Bomarc missile) was a Montreal group originally called the Deltones. They hit #1 in Canada, and #45 in the U.S. with "Clap Your Hands" in 1960. They performed on *American Bandstand* and were the first Canadian pop/rock band to be invited to appear on *The Ed Sullivan Show* (they could not do so due to a scheduling conflict). Unfortunately for them, audiences stopped clapping their hands and the group disbanded in the early 1960s.

2. Lorne Greene must have been tired hanging around the Ponderosa, His #1 hit in both Canada and the U.S. in 1964 was "Ringo," a spoken song. Greene's next three efforts; "The Man" in 1965; and "Five Card Stud" and "Waco" in 1966, failed to crack the top 50 on any U.S. chart—*see Chapter 1, Ben Cartwright – Ladies' Man.*

3. Mashmakan's "As the Years Go By" reached #1 in Canada in 1970. "True love will never die" is the second line of the song and may help

readers remember the hit which sold around 400,000 copies in the U.S. and Japan. As the years went by the group did not have another hit, though several members later formed the band April Wine and found success in that guise.

4. "Last Song" by Edward Bear hit the top of the charts in Canada and #3 in the U.S. in 1973. Alas, "Last Song" was their last commercial hit.

5. Skylark's "Wildflower" would likely be best remembered for the mellow-crooned line, "Let her cry, for she's a lady." The lyrics may not have fit well with the times since the feminist movement was topical in 1973. Skylark did not have another hit. Keyboard player David Foster did though. He became a major record producer in the U.S. in the 1980s. By mid-decade *Rolling Stone* had labelled him, "The master of … bombastic pop kitsch."

6. Sweeney Todd had a number one hit with "Roxy Roller" in 1975 (#90 in the U.S.). Vocalist Nick Gilder left the band and mid-teen Bryan Adams joined for one year. The band never had further success. Gilder did though. His "Hot Child in the City" was a scorching commercial success, reaching #1 in the U.S. in 1978.

MITCHELL, LIGHTHOUSE, AND WOODSTOCK

There was a Canadian presence on stage at the Woodstock festival. The mostly Canadian group The Band, played. So did Blood, Sweat, and Tears, led by Canadian front-man David Clayton-Thomas. Toronto's Neil Young joined his on-again, off-again buddies Crosby, Stills, and Nash. Canadian acts that were invited who did not attend were the band Lighthouse and Joni Mitchell.

Grant Fullerton of Lighthouse said, "We were booked to play Woodstock but our manager decided to pull us out because he thought it was going to be a bad scene." Lighthouse's hit songs, such as "One Fine Morning," "Pretty Lady," and "Sunny Days" were yet to come. The hits may have rolled in a little sooner with a boost from the publicity garnered from a Woodstock performance.

Joni Mitchell also had not yet hit her commercial peak with "Big Yellow Taxi." She did not attend Woodstock because her manager convinced her that keeping her scheduled late-night spot on *The Dick Cavett Show* was a better opportunity. Hmm—perhaps that fellow dropped out of the same business school as the Lighthouse manager. Though she never attended the festival, at least Mitchell made musical and marketing hay. She is forever linked to the event, penning the song "Woodstock" that was a hit for Crosby, Stills, Nash, and Young. Mitchell's research consisted of listening to the festival stories told to her by then-boyfriend, Graham Nash.

Learning from the opportunity lost from the Woodstock decision, Lighthouse and Mitchell played the 1970 Isle of Wight festival in England. The crowds at that event were larger than those at Woodstock, proving that the Americans do not always have the biggest of everything.

OPENING LYRICS

There were not as many noteworthy Canadian pop/rock singers in the 60–80 era as there are today. Nevertheless, Canadians did provide some memorable songs. This *Growing Up Canadian* quiz provides the first line or two (not including the chorus) of a song by a Canadian artist and the year it was released. The reader's role is to correctly name the song. That might be hard enough. But the author has high expectations so the second task is to name the singer. It is understood that cheating may be necessary. Those who came of age in the 60–80 period are now mature adults so you will not get sent to the principal's office. The answers are found in Appendix A.

1. "Think I'll go out to Alberta, weather's good there in the fall," (1963).

2. "He's 5 foot 2 and he's 6 feet 4, he fights with missiles and with spears," (1964).

3. "When you move in right up close to me, that's when I get the chills all over me, quivers down my backbone," (1965).

4. "Keep your motor running, head out on the highway," (1968).

5. "When you were young, and on, your own, how did it feel, to be, alone?" (1970).

6. "Well, I'm on my way, to the city lights; to the pretty face that shines a light on the city nights," (1971).

7. "You get up every morning from your alarm clock's warning, take the 8:15 into the city," (1974).

8. "The legend lives on from the Chippewa on down, of the big lake, they called Gitche Gumee," (1976).

9. "I cried a tear, you wiped it dry, I was confused, you cleared my mind," (1978).

10. "Could have been the whisky, might have been the gin, could have been the three or four six-packs, I don't know, but look at the mess I'm in," (1980).

PLYWOOD TAKES A CONNORS' BEATING

New Brunswick-born Tom Connors was adopted by a couple in Prince Edward Island and stayed with them until he ran away at age 13. He lived a vagabond existence for years, his guitar being a constant companion. Short by five cents for a beer in a Timmins Ontario bar, he accepted the offer of the suds in return for a tune or two. Connors eventually played more than a few songs (and likely drank more than a few beers) in his 14-month gig at the bar, by far the longest of his career up to that time.

It was in the 60–80 era that Connors released his best-known songs, "Sudbury Saturday Night" (1967), "Bud the Spud" (1969), and "The Hockey Song" (1973). A folk-singer for everyday working people, Connors was best seen in a smoky, rowdy, small-town bar. To keep the beat in the usually noisy beer joints he stomped time with his left foot, earning the Stompin' Tom moniker. After dealing with irate bar owners about the damage done to their stages, Connors began hauling a piece of plywood from one gig to another. The reader is left to wonder how many of sheets of plywood his boot heels went through over the years.

POURING DOUBLE SUGAR INTO A CAREER

Montrealer Andy Kim's birth name was Andrew Youakim and he had reportedly anglicized his name to obscure his Lebanese ethnicity. The song he co-wrote "in about 10 minutes," became an international hit. It is likely that "Sugar Sugar" with its sweetly addictive teeny-bopper sound would have been a monster hit whoever sang it. Naming the band as a group of cartoon characters—the Archies, simply sealed the bubble-gummer deal. Lest the reader scoff at the buying power of the teeny-bopper set, the song was the #1 hit of 1969. It edged out #2 "Aquarius/Let the Sunshine In" and was much further up the list than songs such as Neil Diamond's "Sweet Caroline" (#22) and the Beatles' "Get Back" (#25). Kim was no one-hit wonder. His follow-up 1969 hit, "Baby I Love You," topped the charts in Canada and reached the top ten in the United States. The man was on a roll, fed by a sugar-induced high of record sales.

Continued success was challenging. Teenyboppers grow older. A twelve-year-old has different musical tastes than a person edging past twenty. Kim's 1974 "Rock Me Gently" topped his earlier solo success and had a slightly more adult sound. It reached number one in the U.S. and stayed there for several weeks. As with many in the pure-pop maelstrom, continued success was difficult to achieve. Kim turned to more adult oriented music later in his career under the pseudonym, Baron Longfellow—*see Chapter 4, Flirtatious Webs of the Teen Kind.*

QUÉBEC AND CHARLEBOIS

Complex would barely begin to scratch the surface of legendary Québecois performer Robert Charlebois in the 1970s. He was part of a Québec cultural trinity of Guy Lafleur in sports and René Lévesque in politics. According to Benoit L' Herbier, Charlebois had, by 1974, become "The nerve centre around which all other (*chansons*) gravitate ... he belongs to this new generation which wants to sing about ... Québec as it is."

Though linked with Québec nationalism, Charlebois could be unpredictable and scathing. At a 1969 concert he asked the separatists (or nationalists depending on one's point of view) in the crowd to stand. When most of the audience heeded his words Charlebois barked, "That's why we'll never be free! You're a bunch of sheep!"

Often performing in a Montreal Canadiens jersey and using lyrics written in *joual*, a working-class Montreal vernacular, he had significant success in Québec. Part nationalist and sometime federalist, he had the soul of a folk singer (the Dylan of Québec) and the flamboyance of a rock star, never easy to pinhole to any conventional category. Perhaps that explains the dichotomy of *Macleans Magazine* calling him "an impudent separatist" in 1969 and his eventual membership in the Order of Canada in 1999. The man who flirted with Québec separatism was commemorated on a Canadian stamp in 2009; a decision few countries other than Canada would make—*see Chapter 8, Osstidcho Boosts Deschamps.*

SEASONS IN THE SUN

Terry and Susan Jacks were a married couple and core members of The Poppy Family, a Vancouver-based pop/folk group in the late 1960s and early 1970s. They hit the jackpot with the song "Which Way You Goin' Billy?" which reached # 2 in the United States in 1969.

By 1972 the Poppy Family had disbanded since Terry was not interested in touring and performing live concerts. The couple divorced in 1973. That same year he recorded "Seasons in the Sun" in Vancouver and released it after The Beach Boys, somewhat unwisely, did not do the same with their version. The Beach Boys and Jacks were not the first to record the song. Though many may regard the lyrics as nothing more than mindless pop with extra sugar, it was respected Belgian writer and performer Jacques Brel who penned the song. It had been translated into English by another well-respected writer, American poet, Rod McKuen. The Kingston Trio was the first to record the song in English in 1964.

Jacks modified the lyrics to the point where they are quite different from the original Brel composition. His version of the song with its catchy chorus, "We had joy, we had fun, we had seasons in the sun, but the hills that we climbed were just seasons out of time," was an instant hit. It topped the charts in the United States and sold over 11 million copies worldwide. There was no doubt that after that commercial windfall Jacks could spend winter months in the tropical sun rather than the grey skies and never-ending rain of Vancouver. Instead, he veered away from the music industry in the late 1970s and became an ardent environmentalist who has been recognized with several awards for his efforts.

SNOWBIRD SPARKS MURRAY'S APPEAL

A fortune-telling medium may have predicted that a young woman named Anne Murray crooning in the chorus of CBC TV's *Singalong Jubilee* in the late 1960s would go on to sell 55 million record albums worldwide. Any common-sensical skeptic may have replied in caustic tone that the chances of that level of success for Ms. Murray would be as likely as a black man being elected President of the United States or the Pope converting to Islam. The presidential statement came true of course with the election of Barack Obama. So too did the one about record sales for Murray; a startling result given that she had been rejected by the show's producers a few years earlier and had spent a year teaching Physical Education in Summerside, PEI.

The surprise 1969 hit "Snowbird" catapulted Murray to stardom. It topped the Adult Contemporary charts in the United States and reached #8 on the Billboard Hot 100—an initial sign of her crossover appeal of country, pop, and adult-contemporary styles. She spent a good amount of time on American TV, especially on *Glen Campbell's Goodtime Hour.* Her hits were diverse, ranging from Kenny Loggins tunes ("Danny's Song" and "Love Song"), to remakes of the Beatles' "You Won't See Me," and the Monkees' "Daydream Believer." Her biggest 1970s hit was no remake. "You Needed Me" topped the charts in 1978.

In many ways Murray paved a path to the future. More Canadian female crossover artists were to come, most notably k.d. lang (stage name) and Shania Twain. As much as Neil Young and Gordon Lightfoot, Murray was a Canadian musical icon of the 60–80 era. Many former hard-core members of the counterculture who disparaged Murray's music at the time likely see her in a different light today—after all, aging does bring new perspectives.

Unlike many other Canadian entertainers who used domestic audiences as a stepping stone to live and bask in the permanent glare of America's bright lights, Murray kept her main residence in Canada. She has always maintained close ties with her hometown of Springhill, Nova Scotia and has supported charitable works in the area.

3

CHALLENGES TO THE STATUS QUO

When citizens of foreign countries think of Canada, they may regard the national trait as being a gentler version of the brash Americans next door—less willing to rock the boat, more willing to seek compromise. And though Canada has had a fair share of challenges to the prevailing status quo in past decades (Louis Riel, the Winnipeg General Strike, and the Conscription Crises of the two World Wars come immediately to mind), the explosion in communications technology in the 60–80 era provided a new and dynamic vehicle. Showcasing protest, whether from the ridiculous gripes of a loony few, to the legitimate demands from the many, became common. While Canada did experience societal convulsions, the *zeitgeist* was primarily an American one that took on a Canadian flavour when events occurred in the northern half of the continent.

A GAY MAN PAYS A HIGH PRICE

Calgarian George Klippert never intended that his fight for justice would become so politicized. In 1960 he was charged and convicted for gross indecency, a euphemism used at the time to describe participation in homosexual acts. After four years in prison, he was released and eventually moved to Pine Point in the Northwest Territories to work as a mechanics assistant. The tiny community sat almost directly across Great Slave Lake from Yellowknife. Being a damn big lake, it was isolated too, being a 560-kilometre drive from the territorial capital.

Klippert was an honest man. When being questioned about a fire he did not start, he voluntarily admitted to consensual homosexual acts. In hindsight, he may have thought this contradicted the adage that honesty is the best policy. He was charged and sentenced to three years in prison. The court-appointed psychiatrists confirmed that Klippert was not aggressive, nor did he have pedophilic tendencies. However, he was deemed to be "incurably homosexual" and sentenced as a dangerous sex offender. Given that he could never be "rehabilitated," his placement in preventative detention meant, in essence, incarceration for life.

An initial appeal was unsuccessful. A second appeal to the Supreme Court of Canada in November 1967 failed as well in a 3–2 judgement. There was considerable media coverage and public support for Klippert—the penalty seemingly being far out of sync with the offence. Not long after, Justice Minister Pierre Trudeau tabled the omnibus bill that would radically change the Criminal Code. Included in the bill were sections that partially decriminalized homosexuality, reflecting Trudeau's famous line about the state having no place in the bedrooms of the nation. Despite the bill being passed into law in 1969, Klippert was not released until 1971.

In the 1980s George Klippert married a woman (at the time only heterosexual marriages were legal) and avoided the spotlight as the gay liberation movement gained momentum.

AN ICON OF THE BEAT GENERATION

Joining a long line of unconventional writers who lived a relatively short life, 47-year-old Jack Kerouac passed away in 1969. Few people are more linked with a sub-culture than Kerouac's connection with the Beat Generation that coalesced in the late 1950s and early 1960s.

Kerouac described the Beat Generation as those "with little money and no prospects." He and fellow writers Allen Ginsberg and William Burroughs were the literary leaders of the anti-conformist youth subculture that rejected materialism. Engaging in explicit sex and experimenting with drugs helped complete the persona. This description sounds much like the so-called longhairs of the late 1960s. Indeed, there were eerie similarities between the media-termed beatniks and the later hippies. And modern media can do much more than simply provide interesting descriptors of non-conformists. TV even produced its own superficial version of a "cool cat" in the Maynard Krebs character in *The Many Lives of Dobie Gillis* which ran from 1959 to 1963 (the part was played by Bob Denver who later starred in *Gilligan's Island*).

Kerouac's famous book, *On the Road,* was written in 1951 but not published until 1957. Publishers were fearful of the experimental writing style and potential obscenity charges due to the explicit descriptions of drug use and homosexuality. Since today's teens are bombarded with images of sex, drugs, and variations of gender identity, *On the Road* could seem a little on the tame side to them. However, it was more than risqué for the relatively dull mainstream youth culture of the late 1950s and early 1960s. After all, the hip-swinging, leather-jacketed Elvis was as far a walk on the wild side as many in conformist middle class suburbia were willing to take.

Kerouac had a strong Canadian connection. His parents were Québecois who had settled in the northeastern United States. He spoke only French until he was six and did not lose his accent until his early twenties. A previously unpublished work written in French and released in 2016 was titled, *La vie est d'hommage*, roughly translated into the honour or tribute of my life. When describing the work, Kerouac stated, "I am French Canadian … all my knowledge comes from being French Canadian."

CBC FIRES THE FUTURE CEO

Being fired is not normally regarded as a strategy to build a career, except when the terminated individual is ahead of the times. Those Canadians entering young adulthood in the 1964 to 1966 period who wanted to display their intellectual chops may have tuned in to the CBC TV show, *This Hour Has Seven Days.*

The program pushed the boundaries of TV journalism with a news-magazine format interspersed with satirical sketches and ambush interviews. Apparently too controversial for the time, CBC executives cancelled the show and fired hosts Patrick Watson and Laurier LaPierre. A storm of protest blew in regarding interference from politicians. Though the show was not reinstated, the format was a precursor of programming that was to follow such as CTV's *W5* and CBC's *This Hour Has 22 Minutes.*

The TV news-satire format became more edgy in future years. Having been fired by conservative, uptight executives became somewhat of a badge of honour, much like the post-war leaders of newly independent countries boasting of the time they plotted rebellion while cooling their heels in British prisons. Laurier LaPierre was appointed a Senator in 2001. More surprising was the fate of Patrick Watson. He became the Chair of the CBC from 1989 to 1994, thus heading the corporation that had once so-publicly fired him.

COMMISSION ON THE STATUS OF WOMEN

The second wave feminist movement gained momentum and notoriety in the late 1960s (the first wave being the suffragists of the early twentieth century). Stars emerged. Betty Freidan wrote *The Feminine Mystique* in 1963. But she could not compete in the media spotlight with the photogenic Gloria Steinem, who founded *Ms. Magazine* in 1972. Germaine Greer wrote *The Female Eunuch* in 1970 which detailed female sexuality in explicitly graphic terms—hardly a topic for dinner-table conversation at the time (and perhaps not now as well). As Margaret Talbot wrote in *The New Yorker* in July 2014, "Steinem was the more efficacious leader. Betty Friedan wrote a better book. But Germaine Greer seemed to lead the most appealing life."

Canada had feminist leaders too, though none reached the international fame of the three named above. As in other countries, Canadian feminism had leaders who represented a split that broadly divided the moderates who lobbied for women's equality, from the radicals who believed piecemeal equality measures would not succeed without an overhaul of society. In true Canadian fashion it was the former thrust that received more attention and stimulated more change in the everyday lives of women. And in the true Canadian tradition of slow, moderate political and social change, it was a Royal Commission that was at the forefront.

By 1967, feminist activist and later Conservative candidate Laura Sabia had coalesced more than 30 women's groups to pressure the Pearson government into establishing a Royal Commission on the status of women. While this action seems subdued from today's viewpoint, it was relatively radical at the time. Pearson balked. When Sabia threatened a march on Parliament Hill with two million women, he changed its mind. The Commissionaires heard over 900 testimonials. They received over 400 briefs and more than 1,000 letters. The five-woman, two-man members tabled a 488-page report containing 167 recommendations.

Only the most zealous or naïve would believe that all recommendations of any Royal Commission will be implemented quickly. The commission route had always been a good delaying tactic, taking a little steam out of a kettle that was hissing for social change. By the 1980s most of the recommendations; particularly about equal pay, maternity leave, and prohibition of employer discrimination had been addressed. So too had issues pertaining to marital status, including Indigenous women retaining their status when marrying a non-Indigenous man. Some recommendations, such as a national child care program appears to be nearing reality more than 50 years after the Commission's report.

Some future criticisms of the report were justified. Feminist leaders of the day were overwhelmingly well-educated white women. The Commissionaires were silent on the issue of poverty and how it affected women, as if unaware of the problem. In a surprising omission that begs for an explanation, the report also did not address domestic violence. An additional criticism that the report said nothing about gay and transgendered persons is unfair given the time it was written. It was only when the Commission was underway that homosexual relations for certain-aged adults was removed from the Criminal Code—see *Chapter 3, A Gay Man Pays a High Price* and *What's in a Name?*

CONFLICT ON CAMPUS

It is difficult to write a balanced view of 1960s campus unrest in Canada. Authors who were attending college or university in the 1968 to 1972 period are likely enthralled by the youthful idealistic impulses of the time. They can be victims of nostalgia, enamoured with the student zeal for a voice in the operation of what was up to that point relatively autocratic institutions. On the other hand, contemporary authors may regard the late 1960s unrest as somewhat hypocritical. The protestors of the day were usually as intolerant of views in opposition to their own as the authorities they railed against.

With a rapidly expanding economy the mostly white, middle-class students from affluent families could afford to spend as much time marching and protesting as being in class. Youths from disadvantaged and working-class ethnic families were a less represented demographic at university. Despite the boom in post-secondary enrolment, the majority of post high-school youth were not hanging out at a campus.

Few university administrations were spared the onslaught of student activism. While the national attention may have focussed on Simon Fraser University with its American-dominated faculty, or the University of Toronto and McGill, due to media-centric Toronto and Montreal, there were interesting events at other universities.

The Strax affair at the University of New Brunswick in 1968–1969 involved a young faculty member who led a few students in a refusal to show a proposed new ID card. This may seem like a minor issue by today's standards. But at the time it was a symbol of "Big Brother" controlling innocent citizens. The group staged a sit-in at the library and stayed for hours, piling up books on the registration desk and refusing to leave. More than a little heavy handed in response, the university administration suspended the American, Strax. He then proceeded to hole up in his office with several students. Protests ensued. Then more protests. In the end, Mr. Strax left the university and stayed in Fredericton for the next decade, driving a battered VW Beetle and living in a ramshackle cabin on the outskirts of town—*see Chapter 4, Making the Scene in Yorkville.*

EXPLODING QUESTIONS AT AMCHITKA

It seems unlikely that a small unpopulated island near the western end of Alaska's Aleutian Island chain could be the centre of such controversy. It was located closer to Vladivostok in the-then Soviet Union than to Vancouver. Not only did the activity there spark short-term west-coast protest, it would be the catalyst that launched a long-standing global environmental organization.

With concern that high-rise Las Vegas hotels were swaying during underground atomic blasts in the Nevada desert, the U.S. Atomic Energy Commission was searching for a less populated area to test their new nuclear stockpile. They chose Amchitka Island for three underground nuclear tests. The first in 1965 was a relatively small 80 kilotons. The second in 1969 was one megaton. The third was a whopping five megatons, the largest underground explosion conducted by the United States.

Given that there had been a significant earthquake in Alaska in 1964 there was concern about tectonic activity and resultant tsunamis. Vancouver-area protests sprang up like atomic mushroom clouds, especially during the lead-up to the second blast. Leading the disparate groups was the Don't Make a Wave Committee. Joan Baez headlined a benefit concert at the Pacific Coliseum to raise money to stop the third blast, one of the first benefit concerts ever given.

Despite ongoing protests, the second and third tests went ahead. Though there was no earthquake or tsunami, the Amchitka site was never used again for nuclear testing. The Don't Make a Wave Committee eventually morphed into the Greenpeace organization shortly after the third blast.

Amchitka is still being monitored for radioactivity and tectonic rumblings and is slated to become a wildlife refuge in 2025. The fortunate absence of a natural catastrophe may have been the result of sheer dumb luck as much as anything else. Knowledge of plate tectonics was embryonic in 1971. In 2002, authors writing in *Geotimes* stated, "Since then, we have realized that the island ... is one of the least stable tectonic environments in the United States—*see Chapter 3, Split at Greenpeace.*

HAYDEN, HOFFMAN, AND RUBIN

Despite young Canadians being increasingly proud of their national identity, in far-left political culture they followed young American radicals like lemmings. The border did nothing to prevent the counterculture press, and later, mainstream media, from raising America's leading youth radicals, Tom Hayden, Abby Hoffman, and Jerry Rubin, to rock-star status in the protest movement in Canada.

Hayden was a main cog in the Students for a Democratic Society and a leader of the New Left. Hoffman and Rubin were founders of the Yippies (Youth International Party). After the 1968 debacle at the Democratic Convention in Chicago, the three young men, along with several others, were arrested and charged with conspiracy and inciting a riot as part of the so-called "Chicago Seven."

Adept at street theatre to attract media attention, the trio turned the trial into a spectacle. They regularly ridiculed the judge. They mocked the proceedings. They wore outlandish attire. The result was an acquittal on the conspiracy charge and a conviction for inciting a riot. Sentenced to five years in jail and fined $5,000 U.S. dollars (USD), it was the rough equivalent to $42,500 USD in 2023. The judgement was later overturned as a commission found the massive unrest to be a "police riot." Soon after, the threesome went decidedly different ways.

Tom Hayden was married to Jane Fonda for seventeen years and was a California state politician from 1982 to 2000. In 2016, just before his death, he announced his support for the much more conservative Hillary Clinton over Bernie Sanders for the Democratic Party nomination.

Abby Hoffman had a much different life. He was arrested for trafficking in cocaine in the early 1970s. After skipping bail, he went underground for several years. He committed suicide in 1989, overdosing on drugs.

Eschewing formal politics and radical protest, Jerry Rubin married a former debutante in the 1970s and became a wealthy entrepreneur and businessman. He worked on Wall Street and was one of the first to promote the 1980s trend termed networking, which emphasized the building of social contacts to enhance business opportunities. Always mindful of the benefits of media attention, Rubin and Hoffman engaged in a series of debates entitled Yippie vs. Yuppie. There were no reports on who won the verbal sparring. Rubin passed away in 1994—*see Chapter 3, Night of Gastown Chaos.*

JOHN AND YOKO'S MONTREAL BED-IN

Beatle John Lennon was married to Yoko Ono on March 20, 1969. Frustrated with battling immigration officials for entry into the United States, Lennon and Ono decided to have their bed-in for peace at the Queen Elizabeth Hotel in Montreal on June 1, 1969. The stunt fit well with Ono's avant-garde performance-artist chops. Gathered in the hotel room were Timothy Leary, Petula Clark, Dick Gregory, Allen Ginsberg, and Tom Smothers amongst others. The song the group recorded there under the name The Plastic Ono Band was released when Lennon was still officially a member of the Beatles. With its simple, catchy chorus, "Give Peace a Chance" became the go-to anti-Vietnam war anthem and was sung by an estimated crowd of over 250,000 people at the November 15, 1969 Vietnam Moratorium Day march in Washington.

The song's success must have sparked Yoko's interest in furthering her musical talent. Her first solo album in 1970 featured animal sounds and a great deal of "vocal noise" rather than words (not unlike the "Revolution # 9" piece she and John pushed to be included on the Beatles' *White Album*). Ono's album peaked at #182 on the charts. A follow-up effort went no higher than #199.

Yoko's presence at the 1968 Beatle's sessions had to be unnerving to the band members other than Lennon. She was no more than a few feet away from them, often with tape recorder in hand, portraying a dispassionate, almost judgemental countenance. Whether her influence was the main reason for the breakup of the band, or whether she only accentuated growing tensions, has been a source of considerable debate.

For Yoko, there is no question about her role. In a 2016 interview in *U.S. Weekly* she stated, "I had nothing to do with breaking up the Beatles."

LIBERATION VIA VIOLENCE

Thankfully, terrorism, then and now, is an uncommon event in Canada. But from 1963 to 1970 *Le Front de libération du Québec* (FLQ) launched a series of over 200 bombings in their armed struggle against the anglophone "colonial oppressors." The members of one cell kidnapped British diplomat James Cross. Another cell kidnapped, and eventually killed, Québec Cabinet Minister Pierre Laporte. Rather than reiterate what is already known to most elder Canadians, a few details that may have been shrouded by the mists of time might be in order.

On October 12 Prime Minister Trudeau ordered troops to patrol Ottawa to protect people and buildings. When asked about the military presence in the capital, he stated, "There's a lot of bleeding hearts who don't like to see people with helmets and guns. Well, I say go ahead and bleed. It's more important to keep law and order …" When asked how far he would go, Trudeau replied, "Just watch me."

On October 15 a Montreal rally was held with over 3,000 people in attendance. Labour leader Michel Chartrand stated, "We are going to win because there are more boys ready to shoot Members of Parliament than there are policemen." This was on the heels of the FLQ manifesto claiming, "We have 100,000 revolutionary workers, armed and organized." Later, this declaration of supposed facts was found to be pure fantasy. FLQ membership was quite small.

Also on October 15, the Québec government requested federal military support which was granted. On October 16 Prime Minister Trudeau invoked the War Measures Act which severely curtailed civil liberties. It was the first time the Act had been used in peacetime. It had been used twice before. In World War I (WWI) it resulted in the internment of Ukrainian-Canadians who had originated from an area of the Austro-Hungarian empire. It was used to intern Japanese Canadians (as well as some German and Italian-Canadians) in World War II (WWII).

The use of the War Measures Act was viewed positively at the time. Polls showed high levels of support in both English and French Canada. However, Conservative leader Robert Stanfield and NDP leader Tommy Douglas voiced concerns, the latter likening it to "using a sledgehammer to crack a peanut."

The FLQ cell members who killed Pierre Laporte were captured, convicted, and sentenced to between eight years and life imprisonment. There were negotiations with the five FLQ members involved in the James Cross kidnapping. A typical Canadian agreement was reached. Cross was released. In return, with the permission of Fidel Castro, the FLQ cell members were flown to Cuba on a Canadian Forces airplane. They eventually returned to Canada. In the late 1970s and early 1980s they received short sentences with none of the James Cross kidnappers serving more than two years.

NIGHT OF GASTOWN CHAOS

In the late 1960s Vancouver was known as "San Francisco North," it being a haven for hippies, Yippies, and assorted long-hair hangers-on. The mayor, Tom (Terrific) Campbell, rarely missed an opportunity to tangle with the activist and counterculture youth of the day. When he was not trying to shut down the underground newspaper, the *Georgia Straight*, he was busy promoting freeways through Vancouver's Downtown Eastside and supporting the construction of giant underground shopping malls. With a rebellious, undisciplined youth counterculture butting heads against a brash confrontational mayor who won elections by wide margins, something was bound to give.

On August 7, 1971 a smoke-in was organized in Vancouver's Gastown, an area so-named for city pioneer Gassy Jack. Various "ins" were popular at the time; be-ins, love-ins, sit-ins, and on TV, *Laugh-In*. It was organized by the Vancouver chapter of the Yippies, the radical American Youth International Party known for far-left street theatre—juvenile and silly to some, cool and hip to others. If chaotic street theatre was the goal, it was certainly accomplished.

About 2,000 protesters gathered. When the police erroneously believed windows were being broken, mounted officers backed by colleagues in riot gear moved to break up the group. The youth were in no mood to acquiesce quietly. They fought back with rocks, pieces of cement, and bottles. In the end, 79 people were arrested and dozens were injured. A Supreme Court Justice headed a commission that investigated the riot. He noted the Yippies were "intelligent and dangerous individuals," but also criticized the level of police action, concluding that the affair was a "police riot."

Never one to back down from a tussle with the hippies, Yippies and, in his mind, assorted riff-raff, mayor Campbell saw an opportunity when Prime Minister Trudeau invoked the War Measures Act in October to deal with the FLQ crisis. He stated to the unwelcome American long-hairs, "I would suggest that the draft dodgers had better start dodging—get out of here boy …" Little came of the threat. Even the relatively conservative *Vancouver Sun* chastised the mayor for his opportunistic over-the-top reaction—*see Chapter 3, Hayden, Hoffman, and Rubin; Chapter 10, Draft Dodgers Head North.*

ORIGIN OF THE PENTAGON PAPERS

There was little doubt that there was a difference of opinion in Canada about early 1970s whistleblowers. On one hand, the 1970s stereotype of Canadians being more deferential to authority than Americans carries an element of truth. On the other, living next door to the cultural, economic, and military behemoth meant that Canadians could certainly identify with an underdog.

If there was a poll for selecting the poster child for the whistleblower brigade, Daniel Ellsberg would likely receive a significant number of votes. For Canadians opposed to the Vietnam War (and there were many) he was a hero. Leaders in the American military and government regarded him as a traitor.

Well-educated with a PhD in Economics from Harvard, Ellsberg authored a history of the U.S. involvement in Vietnam, covering the years 1945 to 1967. It was commissioned by Secretary of Defense (U.S. spelling) Robert McNamara, apparently without the knowledge of President Johnson. After two years in South Vietnam, Ellsberg returned to the U.S. and continued to have access to the documents charting the course of the war. Adopting an increasingly pacifist position he first attempted to convince anti-war Senators such as George McGovern to release the information. Failing that, Ellsberg stood over a standard photocopier and ran-off the documents—presumably when no others were around and there was plenty of toner on hand. He gave the piles of paper to the *New York Times* in 1971. The newspaper began publishing what has become known as *The Pentagon Papers.*

The documents shed light onto shadowy government dealings, official lies, and half-truths. These included the bombing of neighbouring countries, the falsification of events such as the Gulf of Tonkin incident, the overthrowing or propping up of various South Vietnamese governments, and a general view that the war could not be won.

Not high on the government's Christmas card list, Ellsberg was charged with conspiracy, espionage, and theft. He faced a possible maximum sentencing of 115 years. However, botched attempts by members of the Nixon White House to discredit and neutralize Ellsberg became known to the court. Eventually the charges against him were dismissed due to government misconduct and illegal evidence gathering.

PEACE FESTIVAL GETS A CHANCE

Music was the real language of youth. If the U.K. could have the Isle of Wight festivals and the U.S. have Woodstock, why couldn't Canada grab a piece of the festival pie?

Politicians were wary of rock festivals, especially after the violence at Altamont in California where there were several deaths, including one attributed to the Hells Angels in their supposed role as a security detail. Unable to obtain entry into the United States, John Lennon and Yoko Ono planned an Ontario peace festival that initially did not to come to fruition. Nor did the one planned for Shediac, New Brunswick.

In hindsight, how politicians would be so easily duped in the leadup to the Strawberry Fields Festival says much about either the crafty promoters or the dim-witted politicos. The Mosport Park raceway in Bowmanville, 100 kilometres east of Toronto, was to be the home of a championship motorcycle race with "some contemporary entertainment" from August 7 to 10, 1970. Wary of alerting authorities to the true nature of the event, the music for the Strawberry Cup Motor Race was not heavily promoted in Canada. It was in the United States though, resulting in as many Americans heading for the event as Canadians. Being a little slow on the uptake, the politicians eventually caught on to the plan and the Ontario Attorney General filed an injunction two hours prior to the start of the festival. A judge denied the injunction and the music festival, oops, motorcycle race, was on.

Estimates range from 50,000 to 100,000 in attendance for "Canada's Woodstock." The audience enjoyed acts such as Sly and the Family Stone, Jethro Tull, Ten Years After, Procol Harum, and Alice Cooper. Canadian acts were Lighthouse, Leigh Ashford, Syrinx, Luke and the Apostles, and Crowbar, fresh off their "Oh What a Feeling" hit. Leonard Cohen and Led Zeppelin, were on the bill but did not attend. Not surprisingly, there were no reports of any of the performers racing motorcycles.

PULL UP THE MONEY TRUCK

Mixing an increasing number of disaffected, unemployed, seemingly aimless youth with a slowing economy is sure to cause a big headache for any government. Compounding the problem was that even when a few jobs became available, many employers were less-than-willing to hire anti-authoritarian youth sporting rebellious fashion. This dilemma faced the federal government in the early 1970s. The solution? A job creation program designed specifically for those disengaged youngsters. The name? The Opportunities for Youth program (OFY) launched in 1971. It would funnel money directly to project participants with no government "middle-men." Young people would be directly involved in the development, monitoring, and evaluation of their projects.

Encouragement for innovative project proposals kept the funding door wide open. And many youth groups walked right in. In some ways the program was a much grander version of an earlier one under the Pearson government called, The Company of Young Canadians. Its 1966 mandate was to "promote community development and social change." However, that program was targetted to the less advantaged. The OFY grants were for the youth of every social bracket; and the educated, sometimes radicalized youth, took more than their share of the pie.

Hmm. With a little creativity, distant bureaucratic control (the money was distributed from Ottawa), and loose project evaluation, there were more than a few OFY grants of dubious value other than as a paycheque to enterprising youth who had filled in a few forms. The program had its supporters; mostly young people. It had detractors as well. For some, it was if the federal government had hauled a flat-bed truck to the front door of every dubious youth organization and began shovelling money out the back. Criticism ratcheted upward when news broke that alternative newspapers run by "leftist long-hairs" such as Vancouver's *Georgia Straight* and Regina's *Prairie Fire* received OFY grants. The staff of these papers seemed to enjoy getting under the skin of the local police. They often stretched the bounds of previous standards of editorial taste and promoted demonstrations and the obligatory sit-in or two.

The OFY grants to the two newspapers were eventually withdrawn. However, other similar media outlets, such as Toronto's *Guerrilla Press,* retained their grant money. Their editors were not happy to have met the standards (weak as they were) set by the authorities. Despite their displeasure at not being sufficiently radical to warrant their grant being revoked, the *Guerrilla Press* kept the money.

Becoming a political lightning rod was the beginning of the end for OFY. By the mid-1970s the program had morphed into more standard job creation programs and no longer existed as a distinct funding vehicle for young adult "entrepreneurs" feasting off government money.

SPLIT AT GREENPEACE

Dedication and youthful passion are frequent personality traits found in the leaders of protest movements. Heated debate about tactics can turn into ongoing disagreements. Disagreements can morph into arguments. The arguments often intensify, occasionally acting as a cover for the fight for air time and the egos of those vying for control. Splinter groups can form, then split again. Such internal rancour has affected many protest groups—and that is what appears to have happened between the Vancouver-based Greenpeace organization and Paul Watson.

Watson advocated direct conflict in environmental activism. Many in the Greenpeace organization believed such tactics were in opposition to their non-violent tenet. Watson's confrontational style and his headline-grabbing persona did not help. His strident comments and actions to impede the hunting of harp seals near Newfoundland in 1976–1977 (with French actress Brigitte Bardot in tow) led the 1977 Greenpeace Board to expel Watson by an 11–1 vote. Watson cast his sole supporting vote.

To this day Greenpeace and Watson cannot agree on whether he was a founding member. Watson claims to have been one. Greenpeace will only acknowledge that he was "an influential member." The organization does not comment on Watson's activities. For those outside the environmental-activist world, the conflict may seem more about ego, personality, and minutiae than policy differences. Whatever the cause, given the decades of animosity the fissures have become canyons.

In 1977 Watson formed his own group that eventually morphed into the Sea Shepherd Society. In 1979, in one of the group's first actions, the Sea Shepherd ship rammed into the whaler, Sierra, causing significant damage. Throughout the years, the methods used by the Society would be labelled by some as eco-terrorism. Watson made no allowances for the traditional whaling or hunting activities of Indigenous peoples. He has mocked Greenpeace as "the Avon ladies of the environmental movement." The Sea Shepherd Society is currently based in Friday Harbor (U.S. spelling) in the San Juan Islands of Washington State. Greenpeace has maintained Vancouver as its headquarters—*see Chapter 3, Exploding Questions at Amchitka.*

WHAT'S IN A NAME?

Women retaining their maiden name upon marriage may seem like a relatively insignificant issue today. But in the mid to late 1970s, when the woman was the wife of the Leader of the Opposition and later Prime Minister, it was a hot button issue on the media train. Albertan Joe Clark married Ontario-born Maureen McTeer in 1973. She retained her maiden name and few seemed to take any notice. Then Clark's political career took off. He was elected as leader of the federal Progressive Conservative Party after only four years as a Member of Parliament (MP). Now McTeer was front page news, especially since she had kept her maiden name—a sure sign to some that she was an ardent feminist. McTeer believed that one reason for the obsession some so-called journalists had with the issue was that she was a relative unknown. "The only story they had was the fact that I used my name."

McTeer was an outspoken, well-respected lawyer who was unafraid to voice an opinion. At times she could appear prickly with the press, especially when faced with what she considered to be an inane query, Unused to such behaviour from political wives, some members of the fifth estate offered sage advice such as, "Why not let the press in to do a Ladies Home Journal piece?" Others felt McTeer got what she deserved. "Mouthing off about abortion or rape law or whatever is the kind of thing that got her in trouble."

During a women's lunch in honour of a visit by the Queen Mother to Atlantic Canada, McTeer was receiving verbal jabs from the wives of some Liberals who were calling her Mrs. Clark. Though elderly, the Queen Mother was not unaware of changing social conventions. Nor apparently, was she hard of hearing. A short while later, she gently pulled McTeer aside and whispered, "Don't be bothered by the criticism … good luck *Ms.* McTeer," (italics added). To this day McTeer is the only wife of a Canadian Prime Minister not to assume at least a portion of her husband's surname. Two previous wives had kept their maiden names but added their husband's surname (Harper and Trudeau) when each became Prime Minister—*see Chapter 3, Commission on the Status of Women.*

4

KEEPING UP WITH BEING COOL

With World War II over and Canada in a relative post-war economic boom, bringing babies into the word made sense. When put to the challenge, Canadian adults performed admirably. The post-war baby boom meant that children and teens crammed the schools for much of the 60–80 era. The mass production of the amazing new household device called the television acted as a babysitter and a very effective electronic billboard. Advertisers could reach children like never before through national or local TV programs. The kids did not have money. But their parents did. And many of them had more cash to throw around as the years went by. TV and toys mixed with the increasing prosperity and the huge demographic bulge to create the first era of consumer-dominated childhoods. It certainly would not be the last.

Children become teens who then move into young adulthood. The transitions are not always easy. Adolescence became more of a lifestyle concept than a definitive age. For some in the 60–80 era adolescence continued well into their twenties or even thirties. There were competing needs—firstly to carve an independent niche, and secondly to establish social acceptance and fit into a crowd. At times, any crowd would do.

It seems that many young people in the 60–80 era were forever trying to "find themselves," apparently unable to locate a mirror. Perhaps some never did. They dived headlong into every "cool pool" that came available—from dubious decorating to garish garments; forgettable fads to peace pacifism;

techno-trinkets to loony lifestyles. Some may have found what they needed. Others may have hit their heads on the bottom of the pool once too often.

The following are some examples of trying to be cool during the 60–80 era. The dates are provided only as general reference points.

1960 – ADULTS IN ABSENTIA

During the 60–80 era Canadian children were encouraged to play informally in back yards, empty lots, a side street, or a neighbourhood park. In this impromptu world of play there were no adult organizers, referees, coaches, or rule books. Inevitable disagreements arose. They had to be resolved by the participating children. If not, the game ended and everyone tromped home, annoyed. No one wanted that. So, by a combination of argument and compromise cooler heads prevailed. Resolution was achieved, almost always with no adult intervention.

One example of many such neighbourhood games was Jam Pail curling.

A Canadian child living on the prairies could hardly be skittish about going outdoors in the snow and ice. Few youngsters want to be indoor hermits for seven months of the year. When the kids got tired of throwing snowballs, making snow forts, and skating on the rivers and sloughs, there was always jam-pail curling.

Opportunities were plentiful. There was no shortage of sheets of ice. And most households had jam pails or tins lying around in the basement, shed, or garage. All that was needed was a little weight for the pail that was accomplished by filling it with water and letting it freeze. Some form of handle added a little class. Though the rules roughly followed the established sport of curling, the jam-pail variety was a neighbourhood invention so rules varied from one block to another.

As one would expect, a cool game like Jam Pail curling was unheard of in the balmy lotus land of Victoria and Vancouver. There, skating on a frozen pond or lake ice was a treat that occurred roughly once every ten years and lasted but a day or two.

1961 – A MAGIC TABLET

No child today would believe that the Etch A Sketch would come out favourably in a graphics contest against contemporary computer software. But in the early-mid-1960s it was as magical a design device as any boy or girl could have. Approximately 600,000 Etch A Sketch tablets were sold in the first year at $3.25 (Canadian) each (about $34.00 today). That was a big chunk of change for a toy. But what a toy! A child could design and draw almost at will before eliminating a drawing and starting again. Architects of the day must have been envious.

The drawing's disappearing act came as the child turned the screen upside down and gave it a shake. The lines vanished as if by magic. They had initially been drawn using two knobs. When twisted, they moved a stylus underneath the screen. The stylus displaced aluminum powder thus creating the lines in the drawing. When the screen was turned upside down and shaken, the interior was filled with the aluminum powder which covered up the original line. There were limitations of course. Drawing curves and circles was tough since one knob moved the stylus horizontally and the other dial created vertical lines. And the Etch A Sketch was really a one-trick pony of a toy. If a child became bored with drawing lines, the device was pretty much useless for any other type of play.

1962 – BROWNIES AND CUBS

A little discipline and a lot of gender stereotyping is just what children needed in the 60–80 period.

Brownies were the young versions of the Girl Scouts, roughly equivalent to the Cubs for boys. In the 60–80 era a member of the Brownies (always girls) enjoyed far different activities than would a member of the Cubs (always boys). The origin of the Brownies name can be traced to a short children's novel by Juliana Ewing in the late 1800s, based on British folklore. Brownies were magical little people who worked around the house at night without ever being asked. Though the little creatures could be mischievous, the domestic angle seems pretty obvious. The folklore beings had brown hair and brown skin which accounts for the notoriously drab brown uniforms foisted on member girls.

As for the boys, contemporary eyes would find the following scene more than a bit bizarre, perhaps even a little creepy. Two-dozen boys, all aged about nine years old are squatting on their haunches. They are in a circle, looking intently upward at the adult leader, a man calling himself Akela. Nearby, are two other adults. One is named after a bear, Baloo; the other a panther, Bagheera. The boys have both arms pointing downward. Each hand has two outstretched fingers. Then they begin to chant. The boy leader howls to the cub pack—"Akela we'll do our best, dyb, dyb, dyb" (do your best), followed by the group's cultish response, "dob-dob-dob" (do our best).

The strange ceremony is the Cub-scout Grand Howl, used in the 60-80 era by Canadian Cub troops. The boys on their haunches with their arms down represented sitting wolf cubs. The leader Akela was the head-honcho wolf from Rudyard Kipling's *The Jungle Book*.

Not surprisingly, the organizations have altered their activities and proficiency badges over the years to better reflect the times. In early 2023 it was announced that the term Brownies would be changed to Embers. The membership selected it over an alternative name, Comets. The move was to disassociate the organization's name from any racial connotations originating from the term, "Brownie." The news was welcomed, though some wondered about the Embers name being connected to a withering fire. The organization's leaders thought differently. "Embers are full of potential … they can *ignite* a powerful flame" (emphasis added).

1963 – CARRYING THE MARBLES

How could a child in the early 1960s carry dozens of marbles to school for a variety of cool games and competitions? Paper bags were useless in the rain or when dropped in a puddle. Plastic bags were not yet common. Using one of mom's old purses did not seem quite right, especially for boys of that era.

Fortunately, many Canadian households had a purple felt bag or two (maybe many more) tucked away in drawers and cupboards. For a child, the Seagram's Crown Royal writing meant nothing. How these drawstring pouches came to be in the cupboard was not important. What made the bags special was their colour (a cool purple) and the material (soft felt). The presence of a drawstring that could be tightened to keep the top tight and prevent the marbles from tumbling out was an exotic and much-appreciated feature. There was simply no better way to carry marbles to school and prepare for a game of pots or to engage in high-stakes negotiations when trading the glass spheres. A good day in competition or on the trading floor may have required the acquisition of another Crown Royal felt sack. Parents never seemed to balk when a child asked if the adults could acquire a few more of the nifty purple bags.

1964 – DREW AND HARDY

Picture books were one thing. Then there were chapter books. But what was really cool was graduating to reading a full-length novel. And Canadian children in the 60–80 era avidly read two series of mystery novels. The series had started decades before and had undergone major revisions in the early 1960s, largely to remove glaring racial stereotyping. In an era of defined gender distinction, boys read Hardy Boys books, while girls dived into those featuring Nancy Drew.

The gender distinction was one of the few differences between the two series. They were both created by the Edward Stratemeyer syndicate which was described by the *Atlantic* as publishing "a huge number of books at the lowest possible cost." The syndicate kept all royalties. The writers were initially paid between $100.00 and $125.00 per book, though that dropped to as little as $75.00 per story during the depression of the 1930s. Both series were written by a variety of authors under pseudonyms—for the *Hardy Boys* it was Franklin Dixon; for *Nancy Drew,* Carolyn Keene.

Canadian Leslie McFarlane was the most prolific ghost writer for the Hardy Boys series, penning nineteen of the first twenty-five titles. He was admired enough to be paid $10.00 more per book than the other depression-era authors. He also wrote the first four stories in *The Dana Girls* series under the Carolyn Keene pseudonym. According to his family, McFarlane disliked the Hardy Boys series, regarding writing them as a nuisance. He was paid upon manuscript completion and thus never received royalty cheques. For many years he was unaware of how popular the books had become. His son Brian McFarlane was also a writer, though he is best known for his 28-year stint on *Hockey Night in Canada*.

For those Canadians who came of age in the 60–80 era the basic background of the two series is well-known. The Hardy Boys (Frank and Joe) were helped by their famous detective father, Fenton. They hung around with pals sporting yuppie names like Chet and Biff. All their cases were in and around the small city of Bayport. Given the impressive number of felonies the Hardy brothers had to solve, each depicting a tussle with nefarious criminals, Bayport must have been the crime capital of the North America.

Unlike Frank or Joe Hardy, Nancy Drew did not have a sister tagging along. Her closest cousins were Bess Marvin and George Fayne who doubled as her best pals and provided support and assistance when required. As one literary critic stated, "She is as cool as Mata Hari and as sweet as Betty Crocker." Nancy was an amazingly talented teen. She was an excellent swimmer, seamstress, cook, and tennis player, amongst other skills and attributes. No wonder she reportedly had an early influence on notable women such as Chief American Justice Sandra Day O'Connor and Hillary Clinton.

1965 – EASIER CANADIAN GAME

For a time, five-pin bowling was a popular source of recreation and the local lanes a cool place to hang out. Where else could a young person visit a smoke-filled room and rent smelly shoes? After a game or two there was time to chat up a potential mate, have a soda, or head to the pinball machine to display wizard-like talent.

The Canadian bowling alley would have looked the same as those mushrooming in the United States in the late 1950s. Yet the game was different. Smaller balls, fewer pins, three tries to roll the ball rather than two, more points for knocking down pins—in retrospect, five-pin bowling seemed so Canadian. And it was; being invented in Toronto in 1909. According to the Canadian 5 Pin Bowlers' Association, it was meant to be a less strenuous version of the American ten-pin game. Five-pin bowling was ranked in a 2007 CBC documentary as the fourth greatest Canadian invention, behind Insulin, the telephone, and the light bulb, all of which are justifiably higher in importance.

There were other distinct types of bowling in Canada—duckpin (*petite quills, en francais*) was played exclusively in Québec. Candlepin was a game played in the Maritimes and some areas of New England.

Perhaps it was the lack of hygienic footwear that had a negative impact on bowling's popularity. It may have been the decidedly uncool team shirts that bowlers wore when joining a league. Popular new toys and activities like Hot Wheels for the younger set and a toke or two of Mary Jane for the teens may have been contributors. For whatever reasons, the image of a young person dressed in Carnaby Street mod-style, or a few years later sporting long hair and a tie-dye shirt, did not seem to jive well with hanging around in a bowling alley.

1965 – FLIRTATIOUS WEBS OF THE TEEN KIND

The date listed above could have been any year in the 60–80 era. There was a never-ending parade of Canadian pre-teens (now called tweens) longing to uncover what awaited them in the upcoming teenage years. And in *Archie Comics* he and his pals were there to provide a glimpse into the future. And what a future it was—full of fun-loving hijinks wrapped in a cloak of gushing sentiment and youthful passion. It was as if their teen brains had become short-circuited. Archie and his buddies were nothing more than hormones with feet.

The web was a complex one. Archie Andrews was not particularly handsome or smart, though he did have a cool jalopy. He was especially fond of the rich, pretty, but spoiled Veronica Lodge. She reciprocated his advances with coquettish allure mixed with jealous pique. She was best friends with girl-next-door-type, Betty Cooper. Betty liked Archie but could not match Veronica's wealth and scorpion-like hold on Archie's heart. Despite her wholesome image, jealousy and envy occasionally impinged Betty's judgement as she tried to cause rifts between Archie and Veronica.

Veronica was more than a little appealing. Reggie Mantle liked her too, and he actively plotted and schemed to cause schisms between her and Archie. He alternated between being a friend, a rival, and a foe of Archie. An overt womanizer, Reggie also tried to date Betty on occasion. She always spurned him, only having eyes for Archie. Reggie also had a longstanding crush on

Midge Klump. Unfortunately for him she was involved with the hefty but dim-witted Moose Mason. The big lad often resorted to pummelling Reggie to keep the cad at bay.

While all this was swirling around, Ethel Muggs (Big Ethel) was trying to partner with Jughead Jones. Despite her amorous advances she could not compete with the boy's love of food, particularly hamburgers and milkshakes. And, oh yeah, Jughead was Archie's best friend. Got all that? It was a future only a tween could look forward to with breathless anticipation.

1967 – GIMBY LEADS A BIRTHDAY BASH

Many Canadians who came of age in the 60–80 era have likely forgotten Bob Gimby. They probably remember his centennial song though, written in English and French. Depending on the person's age at the time, the simple ditty was seen to be cool (7–11 years-old), or regarded as juvenile but catchy (22 and older). Anyone from 13–19 years might have secretly liked the tune but felt it necessary to publicly claim it to be "stupid" (teens can be a tough audience).

Born in a town of 300 people in Saskatchewan, Gimby wrote songs and jingles for a living. He was known as the Pied-Piper because he often performed his famous song heading a long line of kids while wearing a green costume and wearing a cape—quite un-Canadian for the time. Perhaps he was a signal that the country's entertainment future would demonstrate a greater level of showmanship.

To test the memory of the now-mature Canadians the first portion of the English version follows. If the reader starts singing along then the point has been made.

> Ca-na-da (one little, two little, three Canadians),
> We, love thee (now we are 20 million),
> Ca-na-da (four little, five little, six little provinces),
> Proud and free (now we are ten and the territories, sea to sea),
> North, south, east, west, there'll be happy times,
> Church bells will ring, ring, ring,
> It's the 100th anniversary of, Confederation,
> Everybody sing!

If a now-elder Canadian is still humming or singing the jingle after three days, consult a physician—or a psychiatrist. You need help.

1968 – KITCHEN MAKEOVER

Young Canadians in the 1960s and early 1970s were not the only ones busting their chops trying to look cool. The lust for status infected their parents as well. "Keeping up with the Joneses" reflected an era of unbridled consumerism that served as a narcotic to some adults. Conformity in music and fashion may have been purview of youth, but adults could get in on the act as well. They had their own type of peer pressure.

What else can explain the rush to pitch out perfectly good stoves and refrigerators with the only flaw being that they were white? These were replaced with appliances featuring the fashionable colours of the day—avocado green and harvest gold. This was hardly an upgrade on style or taste when viewed with the benefit of hindsight.

What was once thought to be cool, whether it be clothing or hairstyle, can be captured by the proud owner in photographs. As fashion changes, the clothing and hairstyles can morph from cool to dreadful. Fortunately, the clothes can be pitched out or given to charities. The hairstyle is easily altered. The photos could be tucked away in a dust-covered album.

Not so with the supposedly cool appliances. High cost was a deterrent to rapid replacement. So, the avocado and harvest gold appliances remained in the kitchen. They were on unsightly display day in and day out, years after the colours had morphed from being so cool to being so mocked. Seen through contemporary eyes few items scream louder about 1970s decorating style than these earth-tone appliances.

There was an even worse colour choice. Some now-elder Canadians may remember appliances with a brownish hue. The colour was usually labelled as coppertone, as if the appliance had acquired an appealing tan from a month outside in the sun. Thankfully, the coppertone hue never became as popular as its avocado green and harvest gold competitors.

1969 – MAKING THE SCENE IN YORKVILLE

Yorkville was not the first of the alternate-lifestyle Toronto neighbourhoods. The Gerrard Village with its Bohemian Embassy Coffee House was as hip a scene as one could find in conservative Toronto in the early 1960s. A young Margaret Atwood read poetry there. Bob Dylan showed up and played a few songs.

Fast forward a few years and the Yorkville area became the enclave for counterculture youth. It was relatively close to downtown and the University of Toronto. More importantly, it was a low-rent district where coffee-house leases were inexpensive and the residential rents were cheap. In the heyday, a person could smoke a joint or two, rap with some dudes on the corner, and then make the scene at the local hang-out coffee house. Performers like Joni Mitchell or Buffy St. Marie might be strumming in the corner, hoping to make the big-time some day.

Nearby was Rochdale College, a branch of the University of Toronto. It was busy with an innovative blending of the previously disparate public enterprises of education and cooperative housing. It was named for the Rochdale Cooperative Society in England in 1844 which was formed at the height of the Chartists—a nineteenth century movement strikingly compatible philosophically with the 1960s counterculture. Rochdale College was tuition-free. There were no structured courses, exams, or decision-making structures. Student groups coalesced around an interest. "Resource people" led informal discussions. Like most of the experimental education movements of the day, Rochdale College existed for a few years and then closed.

The Yorkville vibe lasted much longer, just not as the "hippie-haven" it once was. Once developers started extending the shopping strip along Bloor Street the buildings got newer, the rents heftier, and the locals richer. By the turn of the century the transition was completed to the point when in 2008 *Fortune Magazine* ranked the "Mink Mile" along Bloor as the seventh most expensive shopping district in the world.

1970 – OVERLAND TRAIL (THE)

Thousands of North American youth rambled through Europe in the late 1960s and early 1970s. With flags sewn on their packs and Volkswagen Vans or railway passes as transportation, destinations such as Amsterdam, the Greek Islands, and the Malaga area on the Spanish coast were popular. The more adventuresome ventured further afield to Morocco and Turkey. For the true wanderlust crazies there was the overland trail to Kathmandu in Nepal.

A good starting point was the Pudding Shop in the Sultanahmet area of Istanbul. It was here that young Canadians would gather with western Europeans and Americans, swap tales infused with hyperbole and arrange travel to Kathmandu. The city had an area dubbed Freak Street which made the Haight in 1967–1968 San Francisco look like a nursery school. Government-run hashish shops proliferated, making it a favourite hangout for Western youth seeking escape from whatever was making them uptight at the time.

In 1970, a government deportation order freaked out the hippies and sent them scattering to nearby India or Portugal-controlled Goa. Some moved on to Bangkok and Bali. The Iranian revolution in the late 1970s and the Soviet invasion of Afghanistan shortly afterward made the overland trail more than a tad dangerous for back-packing westerners. Henceforth, the route was best left to rifle-toting guerillas and spies masquerading as international aid workers.

1973 – REAL BOOZE FOR AN ADULT DATE

While the parents may have been downing Martinis, Whisky Sours, and Sidecars in the early to mid-1960s, many youths were sneaking around grabbing a few beers when and where possible. By the time the 1970s rolled around they were anxious to display a little class on a special date when quaffing gallons of the local cheap beer did not cut it. With beer ruled out and wine not yet in vogue (unless you were of Italian or French heritage) there was a need to become acquainted with the "hard stuff."

Gender roles were still clearly defined. For the most part, young men had to foot the bill, except if the couple agreed to "go Dutch." It was not just his wallet that would suffer. With beer out of the question on a classy date, the young man still had to display at least a modicum of manliness. Any type of whisky got high marks on the macho scale, but most young men had a tough time getting the amber liquid down without grimacing. A good old-fashioned rum and coke indicated appropriate levels of testosterone and was at least drinkable.

It was a rare young woman who chose whisky. Sweet cocktails such as a Singapore Sling or a Mai Tai were acceptable, even in a northern winter. A basic Screwdriver (vodka and orange) was serviceable for both genders. If a person really wanted to impress a date and spice up the night, adding Galliano to the Screwdriver turned the concoction into a cool-sounding Harvey Wallbanger. The origin of the moniker supposedly came from a Los Angeles bar where the drink was served to a surfer named Tom Harvey. Thoroughly inebriated, he began running into walls, perhaps thinking that barrier to be just one big surfboard.

1974 – SEEKING STYLE IN THE BASEMENT

It was tough for a youth to decorate a basement pad when disposable income was limited. Posters were a good choice since they were cheap; even free when they were included with a record album. They did not score well on the class metre though. When Canadians coming of age in the 60–80 era moved on from their teens to their early twenties, the basement lair had to exude a less juvenile look.

Hanging macramé from the ceiling was a good start, especially with a spider plant nestled amongst the twisted loops of twine. If an individual wanted to add further glamour to the scene, a funky lava lamp would impress visitors. Brick-and-board bookcases were useful in highlighting a young adult's intellectual chops as long as novels by new writers such as Jackie Collins or Stephen King were removed from the shelves. A bean bag chair was as much a conversation piece as a viable seat. A candle stuck in the neck of an empty wine bottle indicated recycling kudos. It also provided much-needed romantic ambience when the time was right. This was another example of the onset of adulthood. Intimate moments could take place in a locale more comfortable than the rear seat of a car.

1976 – THE BUMP

Some dances are difficult to learn; others are simplistic. The bump wins the award in the latter category. A simple dance works best with simple music. This made the bump a popular choice in the disco era of the mid to late 1970s. It was not a difficult challenge for two adults to collide their hips together. Unlike many dance gyrations, this movement was not particularly suggestive. For most people the hip is not a notable erogenous zone. That may explain the popularity of platform shoes, elaborate make-up, and the truckloads of glitter that made up the glam rock scene in the mid-1970s. When dancing at the disco, if the bump was not going to generate any sexual energy perhaps the clothing and glitter would.

For some people the sartorial garb, as incredulous as it was, still did not raise the erotic scale to desired heights. Seeking a little more stimulation, a few relied on a revision of the dance with the female using the hip and the male the crotch. This "grinding" could claim a much higher score on the erotic scale. It was accepted, even welcomed, at late-night discos. However, no matter how skilled some proponents became, grinding at a family wedding in full view of the grandparents was rarely a good idea—*see Chapter 4, Wrinkle-Free Duds; Chapter 5, What the Hell is Software?*

1978 – WRINKLE-FREE DUDS

The 1950s marketers of the new miracle fabric called polyester boasted that it could be worn for 68 days without ironing, leaving one to wonder if the fabric was washed in that time. Spongy pants made of 60–80 era polyester and its synthetic cousin fortrel could be rolled into a ball. When unravelled it would bounce back instantly to perfect wrinkle-free shape. No more ironing! But the material did not breathe like cotton, causing extreme perspiration and boosting deodorant sales.

In the early 1970s middle-aged and older people took to polyester more than youth. Presumably they were tired of decades of ironing cotton clothes. Thank goodness for common sense as most young men and women chose to avoid leisure suits or double-knit pantsuits.

Then came the disco era. Suddenly the young were wearing stretchy, clingy, unbreathable polyester in garish colours. Blouses and shirts with huge collars were worn overtop wide-legged pants. The clothing was tight in the right places to show off breasts for women, chests for men (hopefully displaying some hair), and bums for both genders and trans-people alike. At the end of an evening of disco dancing the sweat-soaked apparel had to be peeled off. Despite these drawbacks, many late 1970s youth likely regarded cotton as "so yesterday." After all, John Travolta was not wearing a cotton T-shirt and jeans in *Saturday Night Fever*—*see Chapter 4, The Bump; Chapter 5, What the Hell is Software?*

5

MAKING AND LOSING MONEY

It does not take much intelligence to lose money. Given the seeming intellectual shortcomings of some rich business people posing as politicians, it is not a big factor in making it either. In the 60–80 era Canadian firms showed that they could make and lose money with the best of any foreign entity. They could compete in the international marketplace (McCain Foods, Wonderbra), and be innovative (Bombardier). They could be as cheesy as any American huckster (K-Tel) and they could build a significant retailing presence, only to have it disintegrate in the future (Eaton's, Army and Navy).

All the while there was the capitalist-behemoth United States dominating various markets and gobbling up Canadian firms like the munching icon in the *Pac-Man* computer games. There was legitimate concern that Canada would struggle to remain economically independent. The question continues to this day as a new list of gargantuan American technology companies dominate worldwide communication through firms such as Google, Amazon, Microsoft, Apple, and Nvidia.

A WONDERFUL BRA MEANS AMPLE REVENUE

In the early 1960s ample-bosomed women such as Marilyn Monroe and Jayne Mansfield possessed the female shape to be emulated, causing some less-endowed women to stuff brassieres with toilet paper. In 1963, Québec designer Louise Poirier came to the rescue in the form of the Model 1300 Wonderbra Dream-lift; a deep-plunge, push-up bra. It took the lingerie market by storm. A 2007 CBC television series cobbled together a range of celebrities who listed Wonderbra as the fifth greatest Canadian invention, just behind five-pin bowling and one position ahead of the Artificial Pacemaker.

Sales of Wonderbra were impressive. According to an Industry Canada study, bras comprised 40 percent of the undergarment sales in 1960. That number climbed to 75 percent by 1971. The biggest percentage loser during that time was girdle sales which dropped from 40 to 10 percent. The remaining percentage of 1971 undergarment sales was labelled as "other," the likes of which are probably best left to one's imagination.

The makers of Wonderbra, no slouches when it came to marketing undergarments, were quick to notice a preference based on age. Aside from the relatively few who went braless, those coming of age in the 1970s wanted a more natural look. A Canadian professor (Mintzberg) reviewed sales data and noted that, "Young women wanted less bra, not no bra." Eventually Wonderbra introduced the "Dici" in the early 1970s for young women who wanted a natural look, distinct from the push-up of the near past or the torpedo look of the 1950s. The Wonderbra brand doubled its wholesale revenue in Canada in a scant five years from 1972 to 1977. There were imitators in the United States, but it was not until the 1990s that Wonderbra was introduced into that market.

BOMBER'S SALES AVALANCHE

The company founded by Joseph-Armand Bombardier is often cited in the vernacular as "Bomber." The company made the first commercial snowmobile in 1935, producing a tank-like vehicle with skis on the front. Slow, noisy, and cumbersome though it was, the vehicle could transport a group of people at one time. Those inside the contraption preferred the type of travel to sliding or stumbling about in the frigid environment on skis or snowshoes.

People seemed to love the independence and convenience of automobiles compared to trains. This prompted Bombardier to develop a comparative vehicle that could travel quickly and conveniently over the snow. After all, the white stuff covered virtually all of Canada for at least half the calendar year. The company finally developed a small engine that contained enough power to drive a single or two-passenger vehicle. In 1959 the Ski-Doo hit the marketplace. Originally intended to be called a Ski-Dog, a typographical error resulted in the new name. In 1959, 225 units were sold. By 1963 the number was 8,200. Trappers, land surveyors, and ranchers were the main initial beneficiaries. It would not be long before the hunting and herding methods of the Inuit were altered forever as the Ski-Doo replaced most of the dog sleds.

By the 1970s snowmobiling had become a recreational sport, much to the chagrin of wildlife enthusiasts and environmentalists. The Ski-Doo was never going to be a stealth machine in sync with Mother Nature. Excessive noise, significant pollution, and rampant habitat destruction were introduced to once-pristine environments. Not only the wildlife suffered. With no training and often more gusto than brains, recreational users were not always as proficient or cautious as they should have been, then and now. Every year hundreds of snowmobilers break bones, rip apart joints, and otherwise batter their bodies.

Love or despise them, there is little doubt that the Ski-Doo that became so popular in the 1960s and 1970s changed the way thousands of Canadians interacted with their environment in winter. Laws have been enacted to control Ski-Doo use and reduce environmental harm. The vast snowy wilderness obviously makes external enforcement virtually impossible, leaving self-regulation the key to any success.

COUPE MEETS MUSCLE CAR

From spectacular flop to record success—that was the story of the introduction of two lines of automobiles produced by the Ford Motor Company in the early and mid-1960s.

The Edsel launch was a disaster. After a copious amount of marketing research, the supposed car of the future was developed and hyped. It stayed in production for a truly forgettable two years. The canyon-like chasm between the outlandish promotion and the car's price tag was too big to cross.

The Ford Mustang was an entirely different matter. The 1962 design team was led by Lee Iacocca. By the middle of 1964 the car was introduced with very little market research. One did not have to be an arithmetic genius to realize that the demographics in Canada and the United States were favourable. The first wave of those youth coming of age in the 60–80 era was entering the car-buying years. Hitting the sweet spot between a coupe and a muscle car, the Mustang was the most successful automobile launch since the Model A in 1927. This was due, in large part, to its popularity with the younger generation. The Mustang's 1965 list price was approximately $3,000 Canadian (about 27,000 in 2023 dollars). With a relatively inexpensive price tag and a cool-looking body freame, the Mustang was, according to a 1965 ad, "a car to make weak men strong and strong men invincible."

DISCOUNTERS MEET THEIR MATCH

Before Dollarama, even before Wal Mart came to Canada (1994), there were low-priced retailers that at one time could boast customers from a surprisingly broad demographic.

Army and Navy opened its first store in Vancouver in 1919, selling surplus army and navy goods from World War I. By 1920 a store had opened in Regina and another in Edmonton, eight years later. More stores were to follow—Moose Jaw, New Westminster, another in Edmonton, Saskatoon (1973), and Calgary (1980). It was a rare woman or teenage girl in those cities in the 1950s to 1970s who did not have at least one foray into the chaotic madhouse known simply as, "the shoe sale." There, she would push and jostle fellow bargain hunters foraging through the racks and bins, hoping to nab the perfect pair of shoes at rock-bottom prices.

The popularity continued in the late 1960s and 1970s. The north-side Edmonton store was enlarged in 1968; the Regina store a year later. The purchase of an Eaton's location in Saskatoon in 1973 kept the expansion going. So did a store opening in Calgary in 1980, the latter the first to be located inside a shopping mall.

Another Canadian discount retailer was having its heyday in the 60–80 era. Zellers first opened in Brampton, Ontario. From 1952 to 1976 the Canadian chain grew from revenues of $27 million in 35 stores to $407 million across 155 outlets. It made an astute and aggressive move into many suburban locations in the 1960s. With the slogan, "The lowest price is the law," the mascot Zeddy, and those cool, and for the time, innovative Club Z points, Zellers was a mainstay of the Canadian retail landscape.

Fields attempted to buy the Zellers chain in 1976. After some deft corporate shenanigans, the tables were turned. Zellers added 70 Fields stores (and several Marshall Wells ones as well) to the fold. Then history repeated itself two years later. Only this time, Zellers was on the receiving end. It attempted to buy the Hudson's Bay Company. But, in a twist of fate, Zellers became the victim and the Bay bought it! You just cannot make this stuff up! The Zellers brand name was retained since the two chains appealed to a different demographic.

Alas, Zellers and Army and Navy could not withstand the introduction into the Canadian market of the American giants, first Wal Mart, and later Costco. Amazon and the advent of online shopping helped put another nail in the coffin. A new Canadian discounter, Dollarama, added another. Army and Navy and Zellers officially closed the last of their operations in the same year, 2020. However, beginning in 2023 Zellers will once again hit the retail scene, this time having outlets located *inside* Hudson's Bay stores.

FRENCH-FRY KINGS

Some people attempt to corner the silver market. Others strive to be the dominant player in the toy industry. Still others like the sound of the "Carpet King." One Canadian company did its best to be the leading player in the French-fry business, turning a small operation into a giant conglomerate during the 60–80 era. Canadians really could compete in the global marketplace, at least in producing and marketing the less-than-glamorous potato.

Anyone who has walked by the frozen foods section of a grocery store from St. John's to Victoria and Windsor to Yellowknife is familiar with McCain Foods. Who knew the lowly potato could ride the frozen food boom of the 1960s and 1970s into a conglomerate with sales of $10 billion in over 150 countries? The *Globe and Mail* noted that McCain Foods had cornered one-third of the world French-fry market. And all this from a start in Florenceville, New Brunswick. Canadians can join worldwide customers coming of age in the 60–80 era in thanking the McCain brothers for a few extra inches (the measurement of the day) around their waistlines.

Siblings Wallace and Harrison used $100,000 of inheritance money from a family-run seed potato business to start the company in 1957 with 30 employees. Homespun and as earthy as the spud they sold, former New Brunswick Premier Frank McKenna noted that if the brothers were ever prevented from cussing they would become functionally illiterate.

In a very public spat, the family fought over succession and ended up in court in 1993. Wallace lost. Rather than stash his big pile of money in the mattress and get a good sleep, he partnered with the Ontario Teachers' Pension Fund and bought the struggling 140-year-old Maple Leaf Foods company in 1995.

GWG AND THE URBANITE JEAN

From an original market made up of calloused-handed cowpokes, labourers, and farmhands to todays designer-crazed, affluent urbanites, blue jeans have come a very long way. It was the youth of the 60–80 era who would initiate the transition—and a Canadian company was part of the transformational shift.

The Great Western Garment Company (GWG) began production in Edmonton in 1911. With a motto of, "They wear longer because they're made tougher," there was little doubt the target market was similar to American blue jean manufacturer Levi's which had been founded in the 1850s. According to the Levi Straus company, it was GWG employee Donald Freeland who invented the technique of stone-washing denim that produced a more pliable fabric and a softer look. Others also claimed credit. No matter who deserved the glory, with the more malleable fabric and subdued look, the blue jean was ready to make a move off the farm and away from the mill.

No company cashed in more than Levi's. It went from a 15 salesperson, two-plant operation in 1946 to, according to an *American Heritage* article, a 1978 firm with 22,000 sales employees in 50 plants across 35 countries. In 1961 Levi's purchased 75 percent of GWG and kept the price of the Canadian jeans at roughly two-thirds that of the American model. GWG had about 30 percent of Canadian jean sales when it became fully controlled by Levi's in 1972. Even after the corporate takeover the separate GWG label was retained.

The counterculture generation of the late 1960s and early 1970s adopted blue jeans as a kind of uniform, as distinct for them as the suit and tie was for the businessmen of the day. In the early to mid-1960s blue jeans had such a distinctly rebellious cachet that GWG initiated coloured denim so youth could circumvent any bans issued by over-zealous principals against wearing blue jeans at school.

Once almost exclusively for poor hard-working cowpokes and laborers, jeans transformed into a fashion statement for the "greasers" of the late 1950s and early 1960s. Soon after they became the uniform for middle class youth. By the late 1960s, those sporting the denim look were often college-educated young people with enough time and money on their hands to attend music festivals and lounge about in parks and city plazas rapping with their buddies. Proclaiming individuality and rebellion from conformity, virtually all of them wore blue jeans each and every day.

INVESTMENT MADE EASY

If a retail investor (a term for a non-professional) has a few dollars on the sidelines in 2023 the options are seemingly endless. There is the stock market, where an investor no longer needs to buy shares in 100 increments—a common requirement in the 60–80 era. There is easy access to American, European, and Asian exchanges, either through a home computer or from one of the hundreds of investment firms more than willing to assist—for a fee of course.

If one does not like choosing individual stocks, there are Mutual Funds and Exchange Traded Funds (ETFs). Both are popular investment vehicles. The Royal Bank of Canada alone listed over 310 mutual funds and 200 ETFs in early 2023. If a person craves more financial adventure there are always call options, hedged funds, or taking a gamble on soybean futures.

This plethora of options rarely crossed the mind of the average Canadian (young or old) through much of the 60–80 era. Even when the bank account was showing a healthy level of cash, many Canadians bided their time and waited. There was always the annual autumn announcement about Canada Savings Bonds.

Canada Savings Bonds (CSBs) were introduced in 1946. Essentially, bonds are a loan from the citizen to an entity, in this case the government. The entity uses the money with a promise to pay it back with interest at a future date. During WWII Canadian Victory Bonds were used to fund the war effort. This new version of savings bonds became available during peace-time.

For many Canadians CSBs were the major, if not sole, investment strategy. They had a ten-year lifespan (later reduced), but could be redeemed at any time. The interest rates were competitive, usually a little higher than a savings account at a bank. They were available once during the year, usually in the fall. They could be purchased in $100, $300, $500, $1,000 and more increments. The toughest decision was whether a person wanted the interest to be paid annually or be compounded. And there were no fees! For the average citizen, there was much to like. In 1987–1988 CSB investment reached its peak of 55 billion dollars.

Canadians must have become more sophisticated and/or speculative in their investment strategies. Citing a continuing decline in popularity and increasing costs in administering the program, the government ended Canada Savings Bonds in 2017, with the last issue reaching maturity in 2021—*see Chapter 5, Vancouver Sharks Circle the Exchange.*

K-TEL – THE KING OF KITSCH

What if a person was walking along a path in an urban park beside a creek or pond and had a sudden hankering to go fishing and snatch a little dinner? How could a person satisfy a sudden urge for a little Polka dancing? How would the demands for hamburgers from a surprise visit of a pack of hungry teens be satisfied? Was there any way a sumptuous salad could be made in a few minutes?

For all these vexing situations Winnipeg-based K-Tel had a product. The pocket fisherman, a record album of the greatest Polka hits (who knew there were so many?), the handy Patty Chef that packed ground-beef into puck-sized slabs, and the truly must-have Veg-O-Matic would have solved all the woes listed above. As the commercials frequently claimed, "But wait, there's more!" There was Bigfoot, a large attachment to a boot so the owner could walk about in the snow making large footprints and spark a sasquatch hoax.

There were Mood Shirts where an oval of plastic in the middle of a T-shirt changed colour depending on the wearer's moods. According to the commercials featuring bikini-clad women, the man's shirt saved him a lot of time on foreplay—it supposedly indicated when he was in the mood (there were no mood bikinis for the women). And wait, there was more—much, much, more; too much to even begin listing the astounding merchandise!

When the compilation album *25 Polka Hits* became a smash hit by selling over one million copies in the United States, K-Tel turned to format albums in the 1970s. Usually based on a music genre like the truly forgettable *24 Great Trucking Songs,* the albums sold in the millions and made K-Tel more money than any pocket fisherman or mood shirt ever did.

One of the first to use the infomercial as a marketing gimmick, Saskatchewan-born Philip Kives remained in Winnipeg as he built K-Tel into a world-wide conglomerate. Perhaps his most lasting legacy is that he demonstrated that supposedly restrained Canadians could rival the brash Americans on the huckster scale.

PROTESTING THE PROFITEERS

In the late 1960s and early 1970s it was not hip to be a businessperson, at least in the eyes of the most strident members of counterculture youth. It was particularly galling to them that a person would seek profit for providing rebellious music. How uncool could a money-sucking dude get? Power to the people meant no more high-ticket prices—better yet, no prices at all!

These folks had to have a pretty poor understanding of basic economics and the monetary motivations of musicians, whether they be rock, pop, folk, or otherwise. Few musical acts, then and now, play very often without pay. Despite this, there were more than a few youths who believed that free concerts should be the norm in the late 1960s and early 1970s. Where the money would come from to rent the venue or pay the musicians was anybody's guess.

The Canadian example of the demand for free-ticket shows occurred during the 1970 Festival Express. Travelling across Canada by train, the likes of the Grateful Dead, Janis Joplin, The Band, and Ian and Sylvia were on board. The festival was to play in five cities along the route. In the end, permit issues resulted in cancellations for the first show in Montreal and the final one scheduled for Vancouver. Only three concerts were held—Toronto, Winnipeg, and Calgary.

At the Toronto event, an organized group of over 2,000 protested the $14.00 advance two-day ticket price (just under the equivalent of $108.00 in 2023). Many freeloaders crashed the gates resulting in anarchic mayhem. It was only after Jerry Garcia of the Grateful Dead promised a free rehearsal that the chaos calmed down.

The next concert in Winnipeg did not have any free-ticket demands. But attendance was only 4,600 patrons compared to the 37,000 who attended the event at Toronto's Exhibition Stadium. An "I want in free" brigade of about 1,000 protesters did emerge at the Calgary concert, held at the ten-year-old McMahon Stadium. Mayor Rod Sykes got into the act, telling the promoter to let the kids in free-of-charge when the concert was well underway. He added a little Alberta flair by calling promoter Ken Walker "eastern scum" who was bent on exploiting young Calgarians. Walker responded by allegedly punching Sykes in the face.

The Festival Express had an initial budget of $900,000, yet only generated about half that in revenue. One does not have to be an arithmetic wizard to figure out that the promoters took a financial bath.

QUICK RISE AND FAST FALL OF AN NHL RIVAL

Canada had pulled out of international hockey in 1970 after complaining about the supposed inequities of its amateur teams trying to compete against full-time "professional" players from communist regimes in the Soviet Union and Czechoslovakia. An eight-game series between Canada and the Soviet Union was organized for 1972 featuring the best against the best.

Well, not quite. In a forerunner to the many machinations that were to come, an arrangement was made between the National Hockey League (NHL) and Hockey Canada that only NHL players could participate. This eliminated four players of the original 35 that had been named to the "Canadian" team, most notably Bobby Hull. Despite a plea from Prime

Minister Trudeau, the NHL refused to budge. Clarence Campbell, President of the NHL explained. "Why should we supply a showcase for our opposition's (the rival World Hockey Association) best feature?" The original, more legitimate team name for the series against the Soviets was NHL All-Stars. The name was not marketing friendly so the Team Canada, easily translatable to French, was chosen.

According to the NHL nabobs Hull was not a "Canadian" hockey player. He had signed with the Winnipeg Jets of the rival World Hockey Association (WHA) for the then unheard amount of $1,000,000 over five years (with extension provisions to 10 years), plus a $1,000,000 signing bonus. Suddenly, in its inaugural 1972 season the WHA seemed to be a serious competitor to the NHL.

Competition in any marketplace is good, at least in capitalist economic theory. For the players the theory became reality. The WHA successfully fought the reserve clause by which players were linked to their NHL teams. Several NHL stars joined Hull by signing with the new league where they found their paycheque a good deal heftier. With the Soviets only too happy to grab some Canadian cash, the WHA organized its own Canada-Soviet series in 1974. Canada had one win in the eight games and managed three ties.

Many WHA franchises had the lifespan of a fruit fly. Though there were many more franchise moves, only those that impacted Canadian cities have been included in this entry. The San Francisco Sharks never made it to the first game, relocating to Québec and becoming the Nordiques. The same fate was in store for the Calgary Broncos who became the Cleveland Crusaders before the season started. The Ottawa Nationals completed one season before becoming the Toronto Toros. They lasted three years. The Miami Screaming Eagles never let out a shriek before moving to Philadelphia as the Blazers. After one season they went to Vancouver. Two seasons after that they went to Alberta as the Calgary Cowboys. The foothills city humanely put an end to the franchise's miserable life after two seasons.

Every franchise collapse put another nail in the league's coffin. It is tough to successfully sell a product when there is uncertainty about where it can be purchased. By 1979 six relatively stable franchises remained. Four: Québec, Winnipeg, Edmonton, and New England joined the NHL—*see Chapter 7, Esposito 1972; Chapter 9, Top Leafs Tossed Aside.*

SALES SLIP AT EATON'S

There are a several once-iconic American companies that dominated the 60–80 era which have since fallen into the corporate trash can—Kodak, Texaco, and Pan American Airlines come to mind. Canadians have had experience with a well-known corporate kingpin which was reduced to a pawn and then unceremoniously taken off the board. If asked to name one Canadian company that could be counted on to survive for the duration of their lives, many Canadians coming of age in the 60–80 era would have answered, "Eaton's."

After all, in the early 1960s Eaton's operated department stores across the country from flagships in major cities to smaller stores in mid and even small-sized towns. Their catalogue was akin to a paper-based facsimile of online shopping. A customer did not have to visit a store to shop at Eaton's. The bulk of paper could also be used as serviceable shin pads for pond hockey games or act as a base for a wobbly leg of a couch or table. In an expanding economy in a young growing country, a dominant retailer could hardly lose.

The future was not as bright as it looked. The Hudson's Bay Company, previously limited to six outlets in Western Canada, purchased Morgan's department stores in 1960, providing it with a presence in Ontario and Québec. An arrangement between Canadian department chain Simpsons and U.S. retail giant Sears provided even more competition, especially in the catalogue business. Sears focussed on car-friendly suburban areas in the 1960s and 1970s. Eaton's continued to operate large stores in the downtown core of major cities—areas that were in relative retail decline in the 1970s. Specialty chains that had never existed before began popping up and picking away at middle class clientele that had been Eaton's' bread and butter.

It would take some time for the Eaton's empire to disappear from the retail landscape. It asked for bankruptcy protection in 1997 and converted to a publicly-traded company. Sears bought the company shares and the leases at several prime locations. It closed or sold the smaller Eaton's outlets. The new name was eatons, with a lower case "e" and no apostrophe, in a rather lame attempt at rebranding. It failed as well. So did Sears Canada which eventually met the same fate as the chain it had purchased. Now, only those who came of age in the 60–80 era and their aged parents can recall the prominence the dominant retailer once enjoyed.

TOUGH GO FOR GULL-WINGED BRICKLINS

Canadians looking for a flashy car that blended luxury with a sleek sports car look had a Canadian-made choice in the mid-1970s. New Brunswick was facing close to 25 percent unemployment. Premier Richard Hatfield wanted the world to know the province was, as he put it, "more than fishermen and loggers." His government offered an initial $4.5 million to support the new Bricklin car company. That level of government largesse eventually climbed to five times that much and would equate to approximately $120 million today—a fair chunk of change for a relatively small province not usually rolling in cash.

The new car was made of acrylic and fibreglass which eliminated potential body rust. It featured gull-wing doors that opened upward. As futuristic as it appeared there were practical current-day issues. It took six seconds for the winged doors to open and another six for them to close. People don't usually want to wait that long for their car doors to open and close no matter how cool they looked. It also made parking beside another car in a regular-sized parking stall somewhat problematic. People aren't that keen on parking at the far fringes of the parking lot to allow enough space for the doors to open.

After three years and only 3,000 vehicles produced, the New Brunswick government refused further financial assistance. In 1975 the Bricklin plant closed and American businessman Malcolm Bricklin returned to the United States. He was not quite finished as the self-proclaimed visionary of automobile innovation. But once again his success was less than fleeting. In the 1990s Bricklin was busy introducing the Yugo to the American market, a car so-named due to the country of origin, Yugoslavia. Not surprisingly, sales were sluggish. There may be even fewer Yugos stashed in far-flung North American garages and fields than Bricklins.

VANCOUVER SHARKS CIRCLE THE EXCHANGE

By the late 1970s those who came of age in the 1960s were in their thirties and may have had a little extra cash lying around. The adventurous may have wanted a tad more financial excitement than buying the forever dull Canada Savings Bonds. In their search they may have eyed the money-making possibilities of the Vancouver Stock Exchange (VSE).

This would not have been a good idea. A 1994 report concluded that the Vancouver market had consistently been "a home of shams, swindles, and market manipulations." The venerable *Forbes* magazine had labelled the exchange "the scam capital of the world." The honorific had been duly earned. In the 1970s the sharks roaming the corridors of the VSE made Steven Spielberg's monster-predator in the movie *Jaws* look like a guppy.

Forbes quoted a 1979 study that investors in VSE companies lost 84 percent of their money some of the time and all of it 40 percent of the time. Anyone dipping a toe into those waters was lucky not to have his or her entire leg bitten off.

The Vancouver Exchange clearly was not going to survive such negative media coverage. The often swashbuckling, sometimes outrageous style of the likes of Nelson Skalbania and Murray Pezim sucked up newspaper print and did nothing to alter the exchange's image. It closed in 1999 when it merged with The Canadian Venture Exchange. The much more reputable Toronto Stock Exchange has operated the Venture Exchange since 2001—*see Chapter 5, Investment Made Easy.*

WHAT THE HELL IS SOFTWARE?

Few now-mature adults do not have at least one story to tell about a missed financial windfall accompanied by a wistful regret of, "If I only knew then what I know now."

In the late 1970s many young Canadians were busy stepping out at new-era discos, wearing their cool, wide-legged, big-collared polyester duds. Meanwhile, a few others, likely members of the audio-visual club when in high school, were getting interested in new-era electronics and were following a few interesting startup companies.

One such outfit began in a home garage. It was a small company with a name only a true electronics geek could relate to—Micro Instrumentation and Telemetry Systems (MITS). It was moderately successful in selling radio transmitters and model rocket parts. In the early 1970s hand-held calculators were becoming a must-have, first for students enthralled with mathematics and physics, and later for the arithmetically-challenged masses. MITS was in on that action too.

On the immediate horizon was a new gizmo that was destined to put calculators to shame. It was an easy shift (at least for electronics nerds) from producing hand-held calculators to developing the new device that was called a micro-computer.

By 1975, MITS had developed the Altair 8800 and advertised the product in *Popular Electronics*, an American magazine well-regarded across North America by those who live for dials and wires. But this gadget was much more than dials and wires. It was a personal computer. Hobbyists were smitten with the software (Altair BASIC) which had been developed by Paul Allen and Bill Gates. While the Altair computer is now an historical footnote, the 1975 software company formed by Allen and Gates called Microsoft did reasonably well in the marketplace.

While mid-decade disco aficionados may have believed software to be a new type of cool velvety clothing, they would have been better off checking what the so-called geeks were gushing about. Putting a paycheque to work buying Microsoft shares would have been a better idea than spending money boogieing under the swirling mirrored balls of the short-lived disco-era—*see Chapter 4, Wrinkle-Free Duds* and *The Bump*.

WOE ON THE FINANCE FRONT

Long before "Hallelujah"; even before he warbled his first song, Leonard Cohen was a poet and novelist. He grew up in the affluent anglophone Westmount area of Montreal and became known as a wordsmith with the coffee-house crowd in the early 1960s. To that point, Cohen's success could only be described as minimal.

Cohen moved to the United States and become a songwriter. The initial breakthrough was a poem that was recorded in song by Judy Collins in 1966. "Suzanne" became well-known and recorded by many artists, including Joan Baez and Cohen himself in 1967. In an unfortunate harbinger of what was to come,

Cohen claimed he was duped into giving up the rights to the song. He became popular enough to perform at one of the Isle of Wight festivals and recorded songs throughout the 1970s (often with Jennifer Warnes). However, his most well-known work was "Hallelujah," and it was not released until 1984. It became a massive hit, though not until several years after its first recording. Thus, Cohen's story in the 60–80 period was not as noteworthy when compared to what came afterward when success and misfortune fell upon him.

As the early decision regarding the rights to "Suzanne" suggest, Cohen's business acumen never reached the level of his songwriting ability. He fired his long-time friend and manager (and one-time lover), Kelley Lynch in 2004. He sued Lynch the next year for $5 million, claiming she had sold much of Cohen's publishing rights and embezzled his accounts and investments. A fellow defendant, Neal Greenberg, counter-sued Cohen. According to the *Irish Times,* Greenberg claimed Cohen "engaged in consistent and prolific spending to support his extravagant celebrity lifestyle." Cohen and Greenberg eventually settled out of court.

No such arrangement was made with Lynch. She refused to respond to her subpoena and was ordered to pay Cohen $9.5 million. She never did. Cohen went back on the road with very successful tours. Lynch responded by sending him harassing and threatening correspondence. Finally, the legal system caught up with Lynch. In 2012 she was sentenced to 18 months in prison and put on probation for five years for what the judge referred to as a "long, unrelenting barrage of harassing behaviour" toward Cohen.

Was Cohen's dire financial situation due to an artistic, creative mind eschewing the logical sequential world of finance? Or was it simply "uncool" for an artist, especially one of Cohen's persona, to be overly involved with business? Was Greenberg correct in believing that Cohen's alleged extravagant lifestyle was unsustainable? These are interesting questions open for debate amongst now older and presumably financially wiser Canadians who came of age with the Montreal troubadour.

6

ON STAGE AND SCREEN

With the language barrier impacting connections to the American film and theatre industry, French-language movie and theatrical producers enjoyed a dedicated though comparatively small audience. With the Québec and federal governments providing support, the province's cultural enterprises operated at a level beyond mere survival.

Federal or provincial government support was not going to create the same effect in English-speaking Canada where shared language made for direct competition with American stage and screen productions. In some artsy Canadian circles "going Hollywood" (i.e., commercially successful) in film-making was almost an affront to what they believed to be the salient issue—to make thought-provoking films. Whether anyone came to see them was beside the point. Despite the views of this small but decidedly snobbish arts intelligentsia, there were some commercially successful northern productions and a few Canadian actors and directors became well known south of the border.

ANNE OF THE RECORD BOOKS

Prince Edward Island is less than one-fifth the size of Vancouver Island. A year after *Anne of Green Gables* opened in Charlottetown (1967) the population was less than that of the city of Saskatoon and around half that of Windsor or London, Ontario. Prince Edward Island had to hang its economic hat on something other than being the birthplace of Confederation and the home of potatoes. Capitalizing on Lucy Maud Montgomery's *Anne of Green Gables* was as good a choice as anything else. To this day, the freckle-faced red-haired girl may be one of the province's biggest attractions.

Don Harron, who played the Charlie Farquharson character on CBC (and later on *Hee Haw*), sent storybook Anne onto the stage when he co-wrote a script and adapted it to a musical based on the famous book. Only the COVID pandemic stopped the theatrical run in 2019 after well over 2,500 performances. The Guinness Book of Records named it the longest running annual theatre production in history. Over 3.3 million people have seen the show.

The musical toured across Canada. It opened in London in 1969 and off-Broadway in New York. The more successful run was in the English city though it paled in comparison to the reaction to the musical in Japan. *Anne of Green Gables* was showcased by Canada at the Osaka World's Fair in 1970. For some reason, *Akage No Anne* (Anne of the Red Hair) became a cultural phenomenon in that country through the next several decades and beyond.

When celebrating the 50th year of production, a son of the co-creators explained the popularity. "It's about belonging, finding our place in the world … it's still something people of any age can relate to today. At first Anne struggles for inclusion, but eventually she finds a loving family … The audience always leaves the theatre uplifted."—*see Chapter 8, A Link From Hoedown to Hee Haw.*

CLOTHING NOT REQUIRED

People may regard a fully-clothed person scanning bodies at a nudist beach as pretty high on the creepy scale. But in the late 1960s and early 1970s a good number of youthful performers did not mind if clothed Canadians paid top dollar to gawk at the bit of flesh they flashed on stage in theatrical productions. To strip or not to strip—that was the question. Nudity on stage and in films not overtly pornographic was a hotly debated topic. Even the pornographic movie industry caught the trend in reverse. *Deep Throat* in 1972 was one of the first of its kind to have a semblance of a plot and character development. It also did not look like it had been filmed with a projector purchased in a second-hand store. Could pornography really go mainstream?

As for mainstream performances, the actors may have found baring one's body in movies less challenging than doing so on stage. Unlike movie-goers, the theatre audience is within easy sightlines of the actor—within earshot too. Picking up an audience member's admiring platitude or ego-destroying groan was possible, even probable.

Some actors either did not mind the attention or needed a paycheque. The 1968 Broadway musical *Hair* contained a nude scene and it opened in Toronto a year later at the Royal Alexandria Theatre. That body-displaying action was in the minor leagues when compared to *Oh Calcutta!* which opened in Toronto a year later. The producers had to recruit three New York actresses to play the female leads since Torontonians seemed unwilling to be naked for long periods of time on stage. Not so with the local male actors. They were either less shy about baring it all or, prompted by male egos, especially proud of what they had to display. Interestingly, as the years wore on, the titillation factor associated with *Oh Calcutta!* diminished and it has not been resurrected nearly as often as *Hair* which even has a high-school version, without, of course, the flesh-baring scene.

FILM AWARDS – CANADIAN-STYLE

The forerunner to the Genies (which have since been merged with the TV Gemini Awards to form the Canadian Screen Awards), Canadian film awards began in 1949. Prior to the 1960s the feature film industry in Canada was tiny, and so were the audiences that watched the product. Perhaps because the pond was so small the competition could be intense. Some complained that the National Film Board won too many of the awards for short films and documentaries. Some French-Canadian film-makers held the view that the awards were unfairly skewed toward English-language productions. Could the movies nominated in the feature film category be considered artistic? At times. Were they culturally significant? On occasion. Were they government funded? Definitely yes. Were they box-office blockbusters? Definitely not.

The feature film category was introduced in 1964 and the first 6 winners were: *À tout prendre* (1964), *The Luck of Ginger Coffey* (1965), *Mission of Fear* (1966), *Warrendale* (1967), *The Ernie Game* (1968), and *Going Down the Road* (1970). There was no award in 1969. None of the above movies were runaway revenue generators. While a large paying audience is not necessarily a measure of film quality, there seems little point in making a film that only a few people choose to watch except to satisfy the artistic ego of the filmmaker. If someone else is willing to pick up the tab (i.e., Canadian taxpayers), so be it.

Two feature film award winners during the 60–80 era stand out, both produced in Québec. The 1971 winner, the National Film Board's *Mon oncle Antoine,* portrays the lives and culture of rural Québec just prior to the 1949 Asbestos strike. Two polls conducted by *Sight and Sound* ranked it as the greatest Canadian film ever made. The Toronto Film Festival, in their poll of the best Canadian films taken only once every ten years, has listed *Mon oncle Antoine* as the best Canadian film three times; a true test of its quality over the decades. In 2008 noted American film critic Roger Ebert called *Mon oncle Antoine*, "a fine film."

The other notable feature film was *Lies My Father Told Me.* It was produced by the Canadian Film Development Corporation and won the 1976 Canadian Feature Film award. And, it was nominated for an Academy Award for Best Screenplay. Though it did not win that award, the movie did take the Golden Globe Award as the Best Foreign Language Film, the only Canadian film to do so.

IMAGE REBOOT FROM CHIEF DAN GEORGE

Born in North Vancouver, an attendee of a residential school, and chief of the *Tsleil-Waututh* from 1951 to 1963, Dan George had numerous jobs before becoming an actor. Having spent only seven years at the craft, he played a minor role as the father in the original production of George Ryga's play, *The Ecstasy of Rita Joe.* So powerful was his performance that Ryga rewrote the part, expanding the character's significance.

George's acting career was bolstered by the recognition he received from his performance as Old Lodge Skins alongside Dustin Hoffman in the 1970 movie, *Little Big Man.* The film was ground-breaking in its positive depiction of Indigenous people. They were cast in a sympathetic light when forced to deal with the nefarious actions of the white men. The depiction of the U.S. Cavalry was diametrically opposite and decidedly negative. The movie was a financial success and received widespread acclaim. George was the first Indigenous actor to be nominated for an Academy Award, eventually losing to John Mills for that actor's work in the film, *Ryan's Daughter.*

Throughout the 1970s George continued to act, always mindful to choose projects that did not demean Indigenous people. The 1976 movie *The Outlaw Josey Wales* was perhaps the best known of the later work. George played the Lone Watie character alongside Clint Eastwood who had the leading role.

A man of many talents, George's 1974 book, *My Heart Soars* was a best-seller that was followed by *My Spirit Soars* in the early 1980s—*see Chapter 7, Chief Dan George 1967.*

JESUS AT THE THEATRE

The conservative church establishment could not be called rock enthusiasts in the 1950s and 1960s. The pounding beat, the suggestive (and later drug-infused) lyrics, and the general anti-establishment tone were but a few reasons for their antipathy. In their minds, if music was to be linked with a stage production, then let it be in traditional musical-theatre tradition with shows such as *My Fair Lady* (1956), *The Music Man* (1957), *The Sound of Music* (1959), and *Fiddler on the Roof* (1964).

By the late 1960s a few musicals were beginning to get a little too edgy for religious conservatives, firstly with *Cabaret* (1966) and then especially with the tribal rock musical, *Hair* (1968). Little did they know what was to come next as Jesus became the central figure in two new productions.

Those coming of age around 1970 were impacting the cultural landscape, and musical theatre was no exception. In eerily similar trajectories two rock operas became popular, *Godspell* and *Jesus Christ Superstar.* Both became stage productions in New York in 1971, *Godspell* off-Broadway in May (it later moved to Broadway in 1976) and *Superstar* in October. Both focussed on the final days of Christ. *Godspell* was based on the Gospel of Matthew. *Superstar* emphasized the rift between Judas and Jesus. Both were criticized at the time for being sacrilegious. They did not include the resurrection, without which, as evangelist Billy Graham noted, "There is no Christianity." Both stage productions formed the basis for movies in the same year (1973) and are now performed in high schools.

The better known of the two was *Superstar* which did receive some surprising high praise from a conservative source. The musical was first released as a double album in 1970 since creators Andrew Lloyd Webber and Tim Rice could not find financial backing for a stage production. Lloyd Webber recalled that he was told that the concept of a rock opera about the last days of Jesus Christ was "the worst idea in history." The Vatican radio station aired the newly released album in its entirety and called it a work of "considerable importance."

The Toronto production of *Godspell* opened in 1972 at the Royal Alexandria Theatre (there was a touring company performing *Superstar* in some Canadian cities that same year). Future Canadian comedy stars Dave Thomas, Eugene Levy, and Martin Short (as well as eventual Canadian Andrea Martin) were in the show. The musical director was Canadian Paul Shaffer who later became the musical director and sidekick on *Late Night with David Letterman*.

JEWISON – THE CANADIAN PINKO

There are few of those coming of age in the 60–80 era who did not see at least of few of the following movies: *The Russians are Coming, The Russians are Coming* (1966), *In the Heat of the Night* (1967), *The Thomas Crowne Affair* (1968), *Fiddler on the Roof* (1971), *Jesus Christ Superstar* (1973), *Rollerball* (1975), and *F.I.S.T.* (1978). The list of movies displays an amazing range of style—comedy, spy thriller, drama, mystery, and musical.

There is a common link however. All these movies were directed by Canadian, Norman Jewison. He was nominated for Best Director for *In the Heat of the Night* and *Fiddler on the* Roof, and for the later *Moonstruck* in 1987. He never won the award. In all, Jewison's films garnered 41 Academy Award nominations in various categories and won on 12 occasions.

Jewison recalled that Hollywood icon John Wayne had been infuriated with the Cold War satire, *The Russians are Coming, The Russians are Coming*. He claimed that Wayne saw "reds under the beds" at every turn and called Jewison, "a Canadian pinko." The director also recalled being forced to escape the "Duke" at a Hollywood party. "The drunker he (Wayne) got the more he wanted to punch me out." Jewsion was not a big man. Wayne was.

Like almost all Canadian film, theatrical, and television personalities of the day, Jewison had his start with the CBC. Also like many others he went to the United States to broaden opportunity, first working in television before launching his movie directorial debut. Despite some criticism from avant-garde film makers in his home country for being too commercial, Jewison kept his base in Canada in the Caledon area of Ontario while maintaining a second home in California. He was instrumental in creating the Canadian Film Centre in Toronto in 1988—*see Chapter 6, New Hollywood.*

NEW HOLLYWOOD

The parents of the 60–80 generation loved biblical epics (*The Ten Commandments, The Greatest Story Ever Told, Samson and Delilah, Ben Hur*). Those coming of age in the 60–80 era likely saw these movies on late-night TV or on the small screen every Easter. Secular epics were also popular as *Lawrence of Arabia, Mutiny on the Bounty,* and *Dr. Zhivago* can attest. Big-budget musicals such as *My Fair Lady, Mary Poppins,* and *The Sound of Music* rivalled the historical epics in audience numbers. The money people in Hollywood believed that historical epics and splashy musicals were the types of films that benefitted the most from large theatre screens. They were the shows that were most likely to lure people off their couches and away from the filmmaker's greatest rival—television sets.

The demographic bulge of youth affected music and television. It was about to alter movies as well.

Sandwiched between the epic-musical era of the early-mid-1960s and the return of the blockbusters such as *Jaws* and *Star Wars* a decade later was a new mini-era of movies, often referred to as New Hollywood. In these movies characters did not suddenly break out in song and dance. There was no multitude of extras waiting to be gored by soldiers or run over by Roman chariots. The films were not three hours long with an intermission for a much-needed bathroom break and another round of popcorn and soda.

These were movies with a new way of looking at the world—*Little Big Man* with Indigenous sensibility, *MASH* regarding war, or *The Graduate* about changing moral standards. The films were sometimes glamorous, sometimes vicious. Young adult stars came to the screen in *Cabaret, A Clockwork Orange,* and *Bonnie and Clyde*. Anti-heroes such as those in the counterculture classic *Easy Rider* were popular, as were the morally ambiguous heroes in several "Spaghetti Westerns," the most well-known being *The Good, the Bad, and the Ugly*.

That this change in movie releases occurred in the 1967 to 1975 period is not surprising. Young adults in Canada and the United States formed a significant portion of the movie-going audience. They were more urban, more educated, and more disaffected than the previous generation. Used to TV shows that were broken into twelve-minute segments between commercials, it was unlikely many young adults of the time could have lasted through three-plus hours of *Lawrence of Arabia*.

Though the reader may groan at the prospect of another snap quiz, take pleasure in knowing that there is no final exam. The following is a list of nine movies, all considered to be significant examples of the 1967 to 1975 New Hollywood period. The task is to name the two or three young emerging stars in each film. The answers are found in Appendix B. Remember, you are old enough to get away with cheating!

1. Bonnie and Clyde (1967) – nominated for Best Picture,

2. The Graduate (1967) – nominated for Best Picture,

3. Easy Rider (1969),

4. Midnight Cowboy (1969) – won Best Picture Award,

5. Love Story (1970) – nominated for Best Picture,

6. Klute (1971) – the lead actress won the Academy Award; a Canadian was a supporting actor,

7. Cabaret (1972) – nominated for Best Picture; the lead actress won the Academy Award,

8. American Graffiti – (1973),

9. One Flew Over the Cuckoo's Nest (1975) – won Best Picture Award.

NUREYEV AND KAIN BOOST CANADIAN BALLET

Ballet would not top the interest list of many youths in the early to mid-1970s. If it did momentarily flash onto the radar screen it was usually regarded as an art form for older people. Ballet was for those who could afford to purchase expensive clothes and head out in flashy cars to sip a few cocktails at a high-brow locale. Few people rode the bus to get to the ballet. The venue was not the local hockey arena. No one was wearing jeans. And the well-heeled audience members did not smoke pot—at least when they were watching the show.

But when a superstar personality put the beauty of the ballet onto the television screen, even several of the youthful masses noticed.

Rudolf Nureyev created an international sensation when he defected from the Soviet Union in 1961. Physically impressive, athletic on stage, and emotionally taciturn with a seemingly brooding personality off it, he had mass appeal. In the early 1970s he connected with the National Ballet of Canada to choreograph *The Sleeping Beauty.* He included two additional solos, not surprising since he was to be Prince Florimund. The production went well over budget but eventually premiered in 1972. Veronica Tennant was in the role of Princess Aurora. Hamilton-born Karen Kain, a relative newcomer to the company, was Princess Florine. Frank Augustyn was Bluebird.

The CBC filmed a performance and it was aired in December 1972. With the lavish sets and Nureyev in the lead, there were many who watched the show who had never seen ballet previously. Adding more publicity was Kain and Augustyn winning first prize at the International Ballet competition in Moscow in 1973 (Nureyev did not attend for obvious reasons). Their performance was a portion from *The Sleeping Beauty.* The Canadian ballet's production performed world-wide, often with Kain as Princess Aurora. It put Canadian ballet on the high-culture map—a different type of recognition for the land of ice hockey and maple syrup.

Though unusually tall for a ballerina at more than five and a half feet, Kain went on to an illustrious career. She performed frequently with Nureyev throughout the 1970s and early 1980s, becoming internationally recognized for her talent. During that time, she was probably the only Canadian ballet performer who had name recognition in the country beyond those who were aficionados of the artful movement. Kain went on to become the Artistic Director of the National Ballet of Canada. In that role she helped produce a refurbished version of *The Sleeping Beauty* in 2006. Nureyev passed away in 1993.

Indicative of how the world of ballet has changed since the 60–80 era, CBC reported that in 2019 more boys than girls were in the graduating class of the National Ballet School.

ON A ROCKY ROAD TO HORROR

The *Rocky Horror Show* theatrical production was amazingly ahead of its time in satirizing sexual liberation and gender roles. The 1973 London musical production was a spoof on the B-level science fiction and horror movies of a bygone era. That the musical was controversial was no surprise. The plot involved strait-laced Brad and Janet who were trapped in a castle filled by, in their minds, a bunch of weirdos. The unconventional hordes were led by Frank 'n Furter, who was known as "the transvestite from transexual Transylvania." The supremely naïve and completely "normal" couple had their eyes opened. Their lives would never be the same again. The effect would be the same for the young adults from suburbia who were in the audience.

Soon a cult classic for young-adult theatre-goers, the audience became part of the show, frequently wearing similar garb as the characters on stage. During the movie version the audience pelted the screen with rice, toast, and cards when appropriately linked to various scenes. The movie version was released in 1975. Like most movies derived from live-action plays, it may not have had the same direct energy as the stage musical. Nonetheless, the audience still received a good dose of the play's humour and farcical edginess. In the mid-1970s, the movie had an exceptionally long late-night run at Toronto's Roxy Theatre, complete with the requisite audience participation.

As an aside, Meat Loaf had a role in the first U.S. stage production in Los Angeles before he went on to release his break-out album, *Bat Out of Hell* in 1977.

PLAYWRIGHT TREMBLAY IN THE SPOTLIGHT

When searching for a theatrical director not adverse to tackling controversial issues and providing a view of the world not often considered by members of the mainstream society, there is likely no better choice than Michel Tremblay. He began his playwright career in the late 1960s and early 1970s as Québec was shedding the conservative church and anglo-dominated "shackles" of the past. Tremblay's plays touched on subjects that for the time bashed against the normative borders, more-often-than-not breaking through them with a crash and a bang.

His first professionally produced play was *Les Belles-soeurs* (The Sisters-in-law) which featured first, an all woman cast; second, who were from lower-class backgrounds; and third, who spoke *joual,* a raucous, working-class version of French. All three aspects were atypical at the time. The play was famously performed in Scotland as *The Guid Sisters,* the *joual* being replaced with language that was described as pungent Glaswegian.

Tremblay's 1973 play *Hosanna* featured a person who at the time would be labelled a drag queen who inhabited a world of gay bars and prostitutes on the fringes of society. One year later *Bonjour, la, bonjour* dealt with incest without heaping the expected scorn on the adult participants.

Tremblay continued to write well past the 60–80 era. As an ardent Québec nationalist, he refused the Order of Canada in 1990. He did, however, accept the Governor General's award in 1999, receiving criticism from fellow nationalists for doing so. He has long opposed bilingualism, calling it "stupid" that a housewife in Vancouver be expected to be fluent in French. Never one to jump into a boat crowded with other passengers, he stated in a 1987 interview that he was a rare breed; describing himself as "a homosexual who doesn't like men."—*see Chapter 7, Levesque 1976; Chapter 8, Osstidcho Boosts Deschamps.*

RICHLER NOVEL BROUGHT TO THE SCREEN

Mordecai Richler's 1959 novel *The Apprenticeship of Duddy Kravitz* was adapted into a movie and released in 1974. The Canadian film was shot mainly in Québec and was nominated for an Academy Award for the Best

Writing/Screenplay adapted from another source. The movie was sandwiched between two prominent film roles for American actor, Richard Dreyfuss. The first was *American Graffiti,* the other, *Jaws.*

Canadian cultural critics of the day had much to talk about. They believed that the film, and the novel on which it was based, displayed a negative stereotype of Jewish people. Duddy was obsessed with status, money, and a parcel of land with which he planned to make even more money. Richler, a Jew, responded with, "To be a Jew and a Canadian is to emerge from the ghetto twice … as self-conscious Canadians and touchy Jews tend to contemplate the world through a wrong-ended telescope."

Some Canadian critics did not like the film for other reasons. It was "too Hollywood" (i.e., too commercially successful). Apparently, a *real* Canadian film was not supposed to make any money. The actors were Americans. This was true. Of the principals, only Micheline Lanctôt, who played Yvette, was Canadian. She did not follow the exposure the movie brought with a move to the United States, preferring to enjoy a successful career in Québec, primarily as a director. A critic from Canada's major magazine, *Macleans,* said, "If acting alone could save Duddy Kravitz, it would be a good film. But acting cannot save a story as thin and threadbare as this."

Why Canadian critics of the 60–80 era liked to pummel home-grown works is a topic for sociologists and social psychologists. Fortunately, in this case, *The Apprenticeship of Duddy Kravitz,* though not a blockbuster in the United States, was noticed. Roger Ebert felt the movie was, "A little too sloppy and occasionally too obvious to qualify as a great film, but it is a good and entertaining one."

SLAPSHOT SCORES ON THE CULT METRE

The movie *Slapshot* was made by American, George Roy Hill, no slouch in the director's chair. He was fresh off making *Butch Cassidy and the Sundance Kid* and *The Sting.* Both those movies starred Paul Newman. Somehow Hill managed to convince the megastar to portray a player-coach for a down-and-out minor league hockey team in in a down-and-out American factory town. But the brawling and fighting in a hockey arena, was, for the time, pure Canadian. When the movie was released in 1977, almost all the players in the NHL and the minor professional leagues were Canadian. Though it was only moderately successful at the box office, the movie was popular amongst Canadian hockey fans of the day. On-ice, bench clearing brawls were commonplace in the early-mid-1970s, as exemplified by the-then frequently heard refrain, "I went to a fight last night and a hockey game broke out."

The raunchy humour of the dressing room was noteworthy. But the highlight was the Hanson brothers, complete with long stringy hair and black-rimmed, coke-bottle glasses. The movie was based on the lives of the players on the decidedly minor-league Johnstown Jets of the soon to be defunct North American Hockey League. The Hanson characters were based on a real-life bother trio who, more skilled with fists than with the puck, spent as much time in the penalty box as on the ice. The bench-clearing brawl they initiate in the film before a game even begins was based on an actual event. So too was their mid-game foray into the stands to pound on a troublesome fan. Hill cast several minor-league hockey players for on-ice authenticity, turning down the likes of Al Pacino, John Travolta, and Harrison Ford for various roles due to their limited skating ability.

Off-beat, raunchy, violent, and undeniably funny in parts, *Slapshot* has become a cult classic amongst Canadian hockey fans—a kind of historical video of the game at the time. As Mike Milbury, former NHL coach and general manager stated, "Some people think *Slapshot* was fiction. It's not. It was a documentary."

SUPERMAN'S GIRL FRIEND

Margot Kidder was probably the best-known Canadian movie actress of the 1970s. Though she was in several Canadian productions in the early years of the decade, she was best-known for her leading role as Lois Lane in the *Superman* movies of 1978 and 1980. Hollywood was a long way in distance and culture from her birthplace in Yellowknife and childhood years in Canadian mining towns like Labrador City. After 11 schools in 12 years, and a suicide attempt at age 14 due to an undiagnosed bipolar disorder, Kidder stayed in Vancouver for her senior high school years and graduated from Magee Secondary.

Trying to carve out an acting career in the 1970s, Kidder completed a March 1975 shoot with *Playboy*. Her career really began to fly when she was cast as Lois Lane in the 1978 movie, *Superman* with Christopher Reeve and Gene Hackman. After the commercially successful though critically panned *Amityville Horror* in 1979 (which the outspoken actress later referred to as "a piece of shit"), Kidder reprised Lois Lane in *Superman II*. It was a character role that would define her career. In a CBS interview upon Reeve's passing in 2004 Kidder said about their relationship, "When you're strapped to someone hanging from the ceiling for months … you get pretty darned close."

In 1996 Kidder had a well-publicized mental breakdown. She recovered and continued to work as an actress, though mostly in minor roles. Following her mother's political leanings (her father was an American Republican, her mother a left-leaning Canadian), she was active in progressive causes. Though she likely did not believe her brother to be left-leaning enough, she did support his ultimately unsuccessful bid as a federal Liberal candidate in 2011. Margot Kidder passed away at her home in Montana, the coroner determining that it was the result of suicide by overdose.

THE CARNAGE OF CRONENBERG

Who would have thought Canadians could make horror movies that would cause audiences to cringe and shriek with repulsive distaste? Who would have thought that funding for several of these 1970s body-horror movies was through a government agency?

Toronto-born filmmaker David Cronenberg's nicknames were "The Baron of Blood" and "King of Venereal Horror." These were strong indications that he was not making movies to rival *Mary Poppins*. His 1975 Canadian movie *Shivers* originally had a working title of "Orgy of the Blood Parasites," so it was not difficult to guess the film's general thrust. His 1977 movie *Rabid* was deemed by *Variety* as "an extremely violent, sometimes nauseating picture." A debate ensued in the House of Commons about the film's savage, sexual nature and the funding provided by the Crown's Canada Film Development Corporation that made it possible.

With a film style labelled as "body horror," Cronenberg was not finished spilling blood from the various orifices of unfortunate victims. *Brood* was released in 1979. Cronenberg was becoming a better director, at least in the eyes of the *Variety* critic who called this film "an extremely well made, if essentially nauseating shocker."

Cronenberg remained dedicated to making movies in Canada. As such, he rarely had the opportunity to work with massive budgets—the films, *The Dead Zone* (1983) and *The Fly* (1986) being two exceptions.

Another Canadian-made horror movie sent audience blood churning at around the same time. *The Changeling* starred George C. Scott and was released in 1980. Though it was set in Seattle, most of the movie was shot in the Vancouver and Victoria areas. The movie had a more traditional haunted house plot to it and therefore was not in the body horror style of Cronenberg.

As the 60–80 era ended, had Canadian film making found a distinct style in producing horror movies? In a reversal of the stereotype of the passive Canuck, were Canadians really that adept at scaring the hell out of people?

WAR-ACE BISHOP TREADS THE BOARDS

Billy Bishop was an ace Canadian pilot in World War I at a time when one-on-one air battles conducted in rickety aircraft were the norm. As one of the top pilots of the day, Bishop claimed 72 victories, though some historians consider that number to be exaggerated. While he helped develop the Commonwealth Air Training Program in Canada in World War II, the two-man musical *Billy Bishop Goes to War* focussed on his role as an ace wartime pilot.

The writers and original actors were John Gray and Eric Peterson, the latter to become more well known via the TV series *Street Legal* and *Corner Gas*. The play opened in 1978 at the Vancouver East Cultural Centre. Bishop, simultaneously proud of his achievements and disillusioned by the horror of war, becomes a conflicted character. One early scene has actor Peterson doing double-duty dialogue as a curmudgeonly Scot and an eager Bishop. The character from Scotland explains to the young Canuck that entry into the Air Corps is getting easier by the day. "The upper classes are depressed by the present statistics so they're not joining with their usual alacrity. Now, anyone who wants to can get blown out of the air ... even Canadians." Later, when explaining his war record of downing German airmen and killing "the Hun," Bishop states, "I go up as much as I can. Even on my day off. My score is getting higher and higher, because I *like* it."

Though well-received across the United States in subsequent years, the initial Broadway opening in 1980 lasted only 12 shows; the off-Broadway production two months. In Canada there has been over 150 productions over the years making it one of the most viewed Canadian plays in history. The Billy Bishop airport near the centre of Toronto is named after the WWI flying ace.

7

QUOTES OF NOTE

People talk a lot. Every day thousands of words gush forth via an open mouth. Choosing the appropriate words when ordering a cup of coffee or yakking about hockey does not put a great deal of stress on the brain. But providing clever insight or compelling opinion on various topics does. When pushed to produce such thoughtful speech the brain can leap into action or lay dormant. When stymied, it can often resort to trumpeting a silly slogan or barking out an insensitive insult when nothing else comes to mind.

People in the public eye are usually talking a great deal. Today, every phrase is analyzed and debated. In the 60–80 era the scrutiny was not as intense. There was no Twitter or Instagram. There were no 24-hour news networks with talking-head experts sifting through every syllable that had been uttered. Still, head-turner quotes were prevalent throughout the era. What follows is a small sampling, listed in chronological order. All the selections originated from the mouths of Canadians.

JOYCE DAVIDSON – 1960

"Must I leave Canada?"

Saskatchewan-born and Hamilton-raised, Joyce Davidson was one of the hosts of a CBC current affairs program. When interviewed in New York she issued a well-publicized statement about an upcoming visit of Queen Elizabeth to Canada, "Like most Canadians, I am indifferent to the visit of the Queen." To add a little gasoline to the fire she added, "We're a little annoyed at being dependent."

The howling began. The Canadian press surrounded the metaphorically wounded Davidson like a braying pack of jackals. The media was representing an Anglo-Saxon view of 1960 Canada, a place where people were eager to remain in the British orbit. A considerable number of fellow citizens thought the opposite, even at the risk of swapping British influence for subservience to the Americans. Interestingly, a poll at the time showed that while 68 percent of Canadians disagreed with Davidson's comments, less than 50 percent (48) regarded themselves as significantly interested in the Queen's visit.

Davidson resigned from her show. Her work in TV commercials dried up. Her children were bullied at school. A 1960 article about her in *Chatelaine* was entitled, "Must I Leave Canada?"

The answer to that question was, yes. Davidson moved to the United States where she worked in several New York-based programs. She eventually returned to Canada and had a one-year TV run in 1977–1978 on CTV. She passed away in 2020 from complications related to the COVID pandemic.

MARSHALL MCLUHAN – 1962

"For certain purposes the whole civilized world is made up of the psychological equivalent of a primitive tribe."

Marshall McLuhan was born in Edmonton and was one of the first to study popular culture from a critical academic perspective. The most influential of his many books were written in the 1960s. His work is not for those with a junior high school education. McLuhan often dismissed his critics with, "You know nothing of my work," a line he delivered in Woody Allen's 1977 Best Picture movie, *Annie Hall*. Though there are relatively few adults who have read McLuhan's weighty tomes, many would likely recognize a term he coined; Global Village, and especially his most famous saying, "The medium is the message."

Both phrases seem to exemplify what 60–80 era Canadians have witnessed as the decades wore on. McLuhan's idea was that the media, not the content it carried, should be the primary focus of study. He likened the media to that of a lit light bulb—it has no content yet it creates an environment by simply being present. Given the dismal state of thoughtful media and internet communication in the United States and the resultant debate about the future of western democracy, it appears that McLuhan's media message was eerily prophetic. So too was his prediction that print media would disappear in favour of "electronic interdependence." Anyone watching the incessant tapping of cellphones by today's tech-addicted teens in the coffee shops of any major Canadian city can attest to the accuracy of that prognostication.

LESTER PEARSON – 1964

"A flag designed around the maple leaf will symbolize … the new Canada."

The Red Ensign was Canada's *informal* flag until 1965. It acted as the nautical flag and in WWII represented the Canadian forces. However, it had never been officially recognized by the Canadian Parliament.

Lester Pearson was convinced of the need for a new formalized Canadian flag. This originated from his diplomatic role in ending the 1956 Suez War for which he won the Nobel Peace Prize. At the time, Canadian peacekeepers were wearing the Red Ensign flag which contained a Union Jack in the upper-left corner. This did not sit well with the Egyptians who raised a legitimate point. The United Kingdom was one of the belligerents. Yet the supposedly neutral Canadian peacekeepers displayed, in part, Britain's flag.

In 1964 the great flag debate was in full swing. Critics, and there were many in English Canada, claimed the issue was caused by "pandering to Québec." Québecois and Canadians not of British descent were more than open to the idea of a flag without a connection to the Union Jack. Over 3,000 designs were submitted to a 15-member multi-party committee. Pearson favoured one with a three-pronged stem of red maple leaves in the middle with a blue stripe on each side symbolizing Canada's expanse from sea-to sea (the Prime Minister and a majority of Canadians at the time apparently failed to realize that the country had an ocean to the north as well). It was assumed that this "Pearson Pennant" would be selected by the committee who would then send it to Parliament for approval. Instead, it was the design of the current flag that was submitted to the House of Commons. The Diefenbaker-led Conservatives were steadfast in their opposition. The rancour and vitriol would make many of today's debates seem like a mild playground disagreement. In the end, Francophone Conservatives and the Créditistes MPs joined the Liberals to force the vote. The final tally was 163–78 in favour of approving the flag Canada has today.

MAUD LEWIS – 1965

"I put the same things in. I never change. Same colours, same design."

Birth defects caused painfully deformed fingers, hunched shoulders, and a chin pressed close to her chest. Bullied and teased at school, Nova Scotian Maud Lewis dropped out at age 14 after only completing grade five. She lived in poverty throughout her life, resorting to using particleboard, cardboard, and even wallpaper as canvas. She never sold a painting for more than $10.00 prior to her passing in 1970. The sales were most often made to travellers on the highway in front of her home. Still, despite her ailment and poverty, she was, by all accounts, a cheerful, shy individual. She also was to become an icon of Canadian folk art.

With no formal training and very little money, Lewis stayed true to her favourite format of bright and cheerful depictions of landscapes, flowers, and animals, particularly cats. For most of her career she painted what tended to sell, even if the revenue was miniscule. Some mid-1960s publicity gained her regional and national notoriety. Even the Nixon White House commissioned two pieces through an intermediary with no evidence that Lewis was aware of the destination of the work. However, as with many artists before her, Lewis became much more famous after her passing than during her life.

In 2003 the Art Gallery of Nova Scotia held an exhibition and 15,000 people attended. They purchased $100,000 worth of Maud memorabilia. In 2022, according to the *Guardian,* one of her paintings that once had been traded for a grilled cheese sandwich sold for $350,000.00. That was quite a one-sided transaction, even when acknowledging the remote possibility of expensive French cheese being lodged between the slices of bread.

PETER NYGAARD – 1965

"Of all the people they were testing … I was pegged to be the president of Eaton's. They hired me on the spot."

At the beginning of the third decade of the twenty-first century, Finnish-born and Canadian-raised businessman Peter Nygaard was in trouble—big trouble. The wide-ranging clothing company he built was insolvent. The criminal charges against him were numerous. They included sexual assault and forcible confinement in Canada, and once that was over, extradition to the United States for charges of sex trafficking and racketeering. The ten children he had sired did not attend his bail hearing. The time being spent in incarceration was lengthening. It is perhaps incorrect to say that sympathy for his recent plight had vanished. It possibly never existed in the first place.

Nygaard was rarely lacking in self-esteem. Just out of university, he had been selected to enter the Eaton's Management Training Program in the mid-1960s, declaring his future in the quote above.

Perhaps miffed about not rising to the top of the Eaton's food chain in his first year or two with the company, Nygaard founded his own clothing outfit in Winnipeg in 1967. Three years later he named it TanJay. He quickly recognized the benefits of cheaper overseas labour, moving the blouse and sweater production out of Winnipeg in the late 1960s to low-cost Asian locales. By 1979, expansion into the United States netted the company $30 million in sales under several brand names—the aforementioned TanJay, as well as Bianca Nygaard (named after his daughter), and Alia.

In Winnipeg in 1968 he was charged with sex offences. In 1980 with rape. In both cases the alleged victim refused to testify. In the 1980 case, later information came to light that the Nygaard company had reached a private settlement with the young 18-year-old. These two Winnipeg episodes may or may not have been Nygaard's first unlawful involvement with women. However, if even a few of the multitudes of similar charges against him over the years prove to be true, it is clear the man was supremely confident that he could get away with anything. And, for a considerable amount of time, perhaps he did.

CHIEF DAN GEORGE – 1967

"In the 100 years since the white man came, I have seen my freedom disappear like the salmon going mysteriously out to sea."

So said Chief Dan George at Vancouver's Empire Stadium, seven years after Indigenous people (known as Indians at the time) were allowed to vote in federal elections without losing their Indian status.

Birthdays can be a time of celebration and a time of reflection. In the speech on Canada Day in 1967 Chief Dan George took the latter approach, reflecting on ways in which Canada's 100 years had impacted the lives, culture, and economy of Indigenous peoples. Delivered in front of over 30,000 people, a small portion of his *Lament for Confederation* speech included, "And today, when you celebrate your 100 years, oh Canada, I am sad for all the Indian people throughout the land … in the 100 years since the white man came … the white man's strange customs, which I could not understand, pressed down upon me until I could no longer breathe."—*see Chapter 6, Image Reboot from Chief Dan George.*

PIERRE BERTON – 1967

"Québecois Flair and English-Canadian Pragmatism"

Coming of age movies have always been popular. The seminal moments in the transition from youth to adulthood always seem to fascinate audiences. Despite the occasional man-child syndrome found in some full-grown males, most adults behave differently than children or teens. They remember their youth with fond nostalgia. Perhaps that is why you, the reader, is spending time perusing these pages.

Can the same be said for nations? Many of those looking back at Montreal's Expo 67 certainly think so, often regarding the event as being the defining moment of Canada's coming of age. Pierre Berton dedicated an entire book to it, *The Last Good Year*, the title being more than self-explanatory. Berton even believed the success of the fair, with its over 50 million visitors, was due to a diminishing cooperative blend of "Québecois flair and English-Canadian pragmatism." Others took a different view, believing that Expo 67 was indeed a turning point—to a more liberal, outward-looking, confident country that formed the foundation of the Canada we know today.

The best group to weigh into the debate are the individuals who came of age at the time. As children and youth, they can recall the Canada as it once was. As adults, they stood witness as the country that has matured into what it now is. It was as if an entire generation had a ticket to a coming-of-age movie with a front row seat in the theatre. They could sit back with a big bag of popcorn and enjoy the show.

JOEY SMALLWOOD – 1968 (as told in Richard Gwyn's, *Smallwood: The Unlikely Revolutionary*).

"I am king of my own little island and that's all I've ever wanted to be."

Joey Smallwood liked to be in charge. He also must have liked jousting and battling in the blood-sport arena that is politics. What else could explain his efforts to stay in power for so long and to keep coming back, time and time again when he wasn't in charge?

The self-proclaimed "Father of Confederation" paved the way for Newfoundland and Labrador to join Canada. Rural support helped to eke out a 52.3 percent vote to become the tenth province in 1949, defeating the independent dominion status favoured by many in the urban enclave of St. John's.

Like a lord with a fiefdom, Smallwood dominated provincial politics for over two decades as the Liberal premier. In 1968 he announced his retirement. Then he changed his mind. His authority was challenged within the party by John Crosbie who failed to unseat Smallwood as leader in 1969. Crosbie left the Liberals, eventually becoming a federal Tory Cabinet Minister in the Mulroney government.

After a narrow loss to the Conservatives in 1971, Smallwood resigned as Liberal leader. He changed his mind again and two years later attempted to win back the leadership. He failed. Now in his mid-seventies and clearly persistent, Smallwood formed the Liberal Reform Party which won four seats in the 1975 election. Smallwood re-joined the Liberals in 1977. By then many of the party members must have been suffering from whiplash as Smallwood came, went, and came back again. He quit politics for good in 1977, finally resigning his seat.

JONI MITCHELL – 1970

"Hey farmer, farmer, put away the DDT now. Give me some spots on my apples, but leave the birds and the bees; please!"

Joni Mitchell was raised in western Canada, spending most of her early years in Saskatchewan and graduating from high school in Saskatoon. Many of her nascent performances were in and around Calgary before moving to Toronto in 1964 to follow her dream of becoming a well-known folk singer. She busked on the sidewalk, worked at Simpsons-Sears, and played in a few church basements and coffee houses. By the time she had moved to the United States, her reputation as a stellar songwriter was at an embryonic stage. In 1967 David Crosby saw her play a gig in Florida and convinced Mitchell to move to Los Angeles. Party goer that he was, Crosby's home was a central hub for the west-coast pop-music elite. Mitchell's *Ladies of the Canyon* album speaks of that time. "Big Yellow Taxi" with its now-famous opening line, "They paved paradise, put up a parking lot," was one of the songs.

Mitchell's line blasting the use of DDT pushed a hot-button issue at the time. The chemical had been used in World War II to control outbreaks of malaria and typhus. With very little testing and analysis regarding potential consequences it was made available to the public. It was enthusiastically sprayed over fields and forests; one notable example being the gypsy moth spraying in 1957. It was apparent, at least to some, that DDT was not very selective in what it killed. While the pests suffered, so too did bees, birds, fish, and quite likely humans.

Rachel Carson's 1962 book *Silent Spring* had a significant impact on the public perception of the use of such chemicals. Borrowing a technique from Victorian England, the book was serialized in the *New Yorker* magazine, increasing the notoriety amongst the public. The story of the tragedy of the defect-causing thalidomide drug broke near the release date of Carson's book, further increasing public skepticism about the safety of drugs and chemicals.

The storm over the use of DDT did not abate, despite the best efforts of chemical companies to denounce Carson and others involved in the environmental movement. The use of DDT was banned in the United States and Canada in 1972—*see Chapter 2, Mitchell, Lighthouse, and Woodstock.*

PHIL ESPOSITO – 1972

"We're trying like hell … and they've got a good team … we can't believe the booing in our own building."

As late as 1961 a team like the Trail Smoke Eaters won the world hockey championship. Only nine years later, the Soviets were giving Canada's best professional players all they could handle. Esposito's 1972 frustrated diatribe in front of a national TV audience was the pivotal moment when Canadians realized that the Soviet hockey players were good—really good.

In the late 1960s Canadian hockey fans grew tired of their national team, made up mainly of university players, being thrashed by European teams. Unable to convince the international hockey big shots that the players in communist Soviet Union and Czechoslovakia were full-time professionals, Canada withdrew from international hockey sponsored by the International Federation from 1970 to 1977. It is an interesting debate as to whether Canada had a legitimate complaint. Most fans in the country thought so. But perhaps the Canadian hockey establishment was simply made up of whiners who could not face up to losing, as many of those in the international hockey community believed (non-communist, amateur Swedish teams were also regularly defeating Canadian squads).

Canadians were confident that the results would be much different in 1972 in the special eight-game Summit Series. This time the Soviets would not be facing college kids. They were up against Canada's best. When Canada scored two goals on the first two shots on a steamy Montreal night it appeared as if the prognostications were correct. A thrashing was about to happen.

A team did receive a thrashing that night—only it was the Canadians on the receiving end, 7–3. By the time the four games in Canada had ended, Team Canada had only one win and a tie. Boos rained down on the team before and after the game in Vancouver, resulting in the sweat-soaked, frustrated Esposito ranting about the fan's behaviour.

It took three consecutive wins in Moscow, all by one goal, to secure the series win for Canada. In the last game Canada netted two goals in the final period to tie the game before Paul Henderson scored with 34 seconds remaining.

For a few die-hard fans the victory meant Canada and its style of play was still dominant. For most others the writing was clearly on the wall. The Canadians won on will, determination, luck, and some questionable tactics. The ice had tilted to even keel. Henceforth, even with its best players, Canada could no longer be guaranteed victory in a sport it once dominated—*see Chapter 5, Quick Rise and Fast Fall of an NHL Rival.*

RENÉ LÉVESQUE – 1976

"I never thought that I could be so proud to be a Québecker." (translated)

There was much to admire about René Lévesque. Being able to coalesce the fractious and disparate groups of the Québec independence movement into a single force with the formation of the Part-Québecois (PQ) in 1968 demonstrated considerable political skill.

In the 1973 provincial election the PQ captured six of the 110 seats in the National Assembly. Robert Bourassa's Liberals won 102. It takes a special level of ineptitude to lose that kind of majority in three years. Yet the Bourassa government managed to do just that. Two monstrous construction scandals, the James Bay Hydro-Electric Project, and the budget-busting 1976 Montreal Olympics, fell into Lévesque's political lap. But much of the sea change was a testament to Lévesque's oratory, his message, and his political skill. In his first term as Premier, the PQ cabinet was filled with university professors and assorted members of the cultural intelligentsia. Anyone who can keep a group like that from incessant bickering has to be admired.

The chain-smoking Lévesque was a walking ad for the cigarette companies. It is difficult for most who came of age in that era to think of Québec politics and not have Lévesque's comb-over hair-style and always-present cigarette come immediately to mind. Political cartoonists regularly drew the

Québec Premier with three or four smokes dangling from his mouth at the same time. A 2010 article on extraordinary Canadians claimed Lévesque's brand to be Belvedere and that he smoked two packs a day. If Lévesque was Premier today, he would be spending more time in the back alley with other banished smokers than he would be in press conferences or cabinet meetings.

Lévesque never fulfilled his dream. The 1980 referendum that asked Quebéckers if they wished to negotiate sovereignty-association with the rest of Canada was defeated by a wide margin of 60-40. A second referendum was held in 1995. Stronger separatist language asked the population to proclaim sovereignty after offering a new economic and political partnership with Canada. That proposal was defeated by the narrowest of margins with 50.58 percent voting no—*see Chapter 2, Québec and Charlebois; Chapter 6, Playwright Tremblay in the Spotlight; Chapter 8, Osstidcho Boosts Deschamps.*

BUFFY SAINTE-MARIE – 1977

"I'm feeding the baby. See, he's drinking milk from my breast."

Saskatchewan-born Sainte-Marie was adopted by Massachusetts *Mi'Kmaq* parents. She eventually returned to the prairie province and was welcomed into her Cree nation in the early 1960s. Writing folk songs and learning her craft, she moved to Toronto and was the quintessential folkie singing in the coffee houses of Toronto's Yorkville and later New York's Greenwich Village. Eventually well known as a performer and songwriter, perhaps what is most notable is her courage to do the unexpected.

To help raise the profile of Indigenous people, Sainte-Marie agreed to appear on a segment on the TV program *Sesame Street* in 1976. Calm in front of the camera and compassionately gregarious with the muppet characters, she was a hit. She appeared regularly over a five-year period. Breaking barriers for network TV, she breastfed her first son, Dakota Starblanket Wolfchild, on air in 1977. Her pal Big Bird was close by, watching intently.

When Big Bird asked, "Whatcha doin' Buffy?" he proceeded to get a lesson on the whys and wherefores of breast feeding and became instantly impressed with his new knowledge of the birds and the bees. A few years later, Sainte-Marie kept crashing through glass ceilings by becoming the first

Indigenous person to win an Academy Award for the best Original Song, "Up Where We Belong" from the 1982 movie, *An Officer and a Gentleman.*

TERRY FOX – 1977

"Someday I'm going to do something like that."

So said Terry Fox the night before his leg was amputated due to a type of bone cancer. He had been reading an article about amputee Dick Traum who had recently run in the New York City Marathon.

Fox was attending Simon Fraser University in 1976 and playing on the Junior Varsity basketball team. A sore knee forced him to seek the medical attention that led to the decision to amputate his leg. He played for the Vancouver Cable Cars wheelchair basketball team and by the late 1970s he had logged more than 5,000 kilometres while training for the planned run across Canada, naming the project the Marathon of Hope.

On April 12, 1980 he dipped his artificial leg in the Atlantic Ocean in St. John's, Newfoundland and began his run. The reception was mixed in that province. There was solid media coverage in Prince Edward Island, but Fox was disappointed in the reaction in Nova Scotia and New Brunswick. There was almost no publicity given to the event in Québec. But as Fox ran through media-centred Ontario, he became well known.

Of course, most Canadians know the story. Fox was unable to cross Ontario's western boundary as the cancer had spread to his lungs. The run ended near Thunder Bay after 143 days and 5,373 kilometres. A TV telethon was aired less than a week after Fox was forced to stop. It raised $6.5 million in five hours, more than doubling the amount raised during the actual run.

Over the years millions of dollars have been raised for cancer research. Terry Fox has attained an almost mythic status as a true Canadian hero. Canada was ready for one. To that point Canada was not a country that embraced the concept of the mythic hero. Perhaps the only other personality anywhere near that level was Maurice Richard in the 1940s and 1950s. But his heroic status was mainly confined to Québec and was limited to a relatively narrow time frame. Fox's ongoing legacy is national, even international, and his heroic status may even transcend the millions of dollars his name has raised to find a cure for cancer.

DAVID SUZUKI – 1981

"When Canada offered refuge … to the boat people, I was particularly proud to be Canadian."

In the early 1970s Ugandan dictator Idi Amin expelled the country's entire Asian population, giving those citizens only 90 days to leave the country. The Canadian government initially insisted that the Ugandan refugee applicants meet the usual immigration criteria. However, the enormity of the crisis led to the rules eventually being relaxed. Approximately 7,000 Ugandan Asians arrived in Canada, the vast majority with business or professional experience and fluency in English. Their integration into Canadian society was rapid. In 1972 approximately 3,300 recently arrived Ugandan Asians were receiving some form of government subsidy. Within a scant ten months that number had dwindled to 150.

The Immigration Act was soon overhauled. Two of the biggest changes were recognizing refugees as a special class of immigrants and including provisions that enabled private sponsorship. This latter point was to become critical during the humanitarian and refugee crisis emanating from Southeast Asia in the late 1970s. Visual accounts of the so-called boat people clearly touched a nerve with Canadians. The country accepted approximately 60,000 Indo-Chinese in only two years in the late 1970s. Particularly noteworthy was the private sponsorship provisions in the new Immigration Act. 34,000 Indo-Chinese refugees were sponsored by individual Canadians, churches, employee groups, community centres, and other organizations.

In recognition of the nation's role in accepting and welcoming the Indo-Chinese refugees, the 1986 United Nations Nansen Award for refugees was awarded to, "The People of Canada." This was a departure from the usual individual-citizen recipients. As of 2021, the special recognition remains the only occasion when the award was given to the people of an entire nation.

FARLEY MOWAT – 1996 (as reported by John Goddard).

"I never let the facts get in the way of the truth."

If there was an iconic Canadian author of the 60–80 era, it was Farley Mowat. From popular children's tales like *The Dog Who Wouldn't Be* (1957) or *Owls in the Family* (1961), to the non-fiction tales of the arctic, few Canadians of the era were not touched by Mowat's writing. In three of his nonfiction works about the north: *People of the Deer* (1952), *The Desperate People* (1959), and *Never Cry Wolf* (1963) Mowat brought the Inuit and the animals of the Northwest Territory's Keewatin district (now part of Nunavut) to the masses of southern Canada in a manner that had never been so influential.

That was until 1996. In an exhaustively researched article in the *Saturday Evening Post,* John Goddard questioned Mowat's version of events and his research methodology. As early as 1964, Frank Banfield of the Canadian Wildlife Service had described Mowat's *Never Cry Wolf* as "semi-fictional."

But Goddard went further—much further. According to him, Mowat did not spend two years in the Keewatin District as he had claimed. It was more like two summer field sessions. Mowat had maintained he was alone. Instead, it was part of an organized expedition. Nor did Mowat ever set foot in an Inuit camp. Nor did he spend months at his wolf den observations, abandoning the work after less than four weeks. And on, and on, and on. Goddard reminded readers that the local inhabitants had derisively called Mowat, "Hardly Know-It."

With predictable tenacity Mowat fought back, launching a boisterous attack on Goddard and his research. Fellow authors rushed to his side. It was suggested by some writers that people did not understand story-telling— sometimes the craft required a little embellishment.

Whatever the truth of the matter (and there remain differing views as to how much "fiction" there was in the three nonfiction works and the veracity of Mowat's self-described research), there is little doubt that the books had an impact through the years. And that influence was bolstered by the unexpected publicity after the Goddard article. Mowat passed away in 2014, retaining all the awards and degrees that had been bestowed upon him.

8

SO MUCH NORTHERN HUMOUR

It was as if Canadian entertainers and writers gobbled humour pills in the mid to late 1970s and caused a sudden explosion of Canadian comedy. There had been a scattering of home-grown success stories—Rich Little, who settled in the United States, and Wayne and Shuster who did not, being two examples. Then, in a span of a few years Canadians exploded onto the comedic scene. Whether they embodied a particular style of northern comedy or were simply talented performers and writers who hailed from Canada is open for debate. What is not at issue is the fact that they achieved a special level of renown—a group of Canadians of approximately the same age who became well-known outside their country at roughly the same time. Never before had Canadians enjoyed that level of success in the entertainment industry. Much more comedic success was to follow in the decades to come with Mike Myers, Michael J. Fox, and Jim Carrey leading the way in the 1980s and 1990s.

A LINK FROM *HOEDOWN* TO *HEE HAW*

Supposedly more sophisticated in their later years, many elder urban Canadians may claim to never have watched TV programs such as *Country Hoedown*. However, given that the show aired on CBC from 1956 to 1965 it is unlikely that at least some now older Canadians did not catch a glimpse or two (and maybe more) of the show when they were children. *Country Hoedown* was hosted by Gordie Tapp for much of its run. From 1960 to 1962 the little-known Gordon Lightfoot was not only a member of the square dance ensemble but also provided harmony on songs. CBC executives eventually wanted a more hip vibe and *Country Hoedown* was replaced by the supposedly much cooler *Tommy Hunter Show* in 1965.

In one of the initial Canadian forays into big-time American television, the comedy duo of Frank Peppiatt and John Aylesworth moved to the United States and worked on several successful TV shows. The Canadians created the show *Hee Haw* for the Columbia Broadcasting System (CBS) as a summer replacement for *The Smothers Brothers* program. They recruited Gordie Tapp of *Hoedown* fame who brought his Cousin Clem character to *Hee Haw* which ran from 1969 to 1971 (and much longer in syndication). Another Canadian, Don Harron, was brought in to play his Charlie Farquharson role. It is up to the reader to determine what level of pride is to be found from this Canadian influence on a decidedly low-brow U.S. network show like *Hee Haw.*

In the mid-1980s Peppiatt and Ayelsworth sold *Hee Haw* to the owners of the Grand Ole Opry for $15 million USD. A financial windfall such as that would go a fair way to put a salve on any embarrassment the duo may have had—*see Chapter 6, Anne of the Record Books.*

ED SULLIVAN'S CANADIAN PALS

Combative during rehearsals and never socializing together after work—it is a wonder the comedy duo of Torontonians Johnny Wayne and Frank Shuster performed together for as long as they did. Stretching several decades, from war-time performances, to radio, to CBC TV, the sketch comedy style they employed became a fixture for Canadians seeking a laugh or two. By the 1970s their style of comedy no longer resonated with younger viewers who preferred more daring and outrageous routines. Canadian TV ratings for Wayne and Shuster specials began to decline amongst the coveted youth demographic.

During their 1960s heyday Wayne and Shuster were enticed to move to the U.S. on many occasions. Instead, they followed Ed Sullivan's advice and remained based in Canada, all the while maintaining popularity in big-market America. Perhaps Mr. Sullivan wanted to keep reciting his favourite refrain when introducing the duo, frequently calling them, "our friends from Canada." The Sunday-night showman had ample opportunity to do so. Wayne and Shuster appeared on his program a record 67 times. Mr.

Sullivan even allowed lengthy Wayne and Shuster routines that often lasted 12 minutes or more, a lifetime for a fast-paced variety show like his. After singer Eartha Kitt's song had once been cut to allow time for a Wayne and Shuster skit, the American singer reportedly asked the Canadian boys, "What have you guys got on Sullivan?"

LITTLE MAKES GOOD IMPRESSION

According to *Wikipedia*, Ottawa-born Rich Little was the pre-eminent impressionist in the 1960s. The eventual "man of a thousand voices" must have a been a royal pain in the butt to any teacher without a sense of humour. He mimicked his teacher's voice when responding to in-class questions. When not doing impressions of his instructors, he was working at the Elgin Movie Theatre as an usher (elder Canadians may remember those flashlight-toting teens helping customers find a seat). He stood at the rear, trying to perfect the voices of those on the screen.

Little's comedy album *My Fellow Canadians* made him popular in the home country. He got his big break in the United States in 1964 with a guest spot on the short-lived *Judy Garland Show*. Canadians Ed Peppiatt and John Aylesworth were established in American TV circles and provided early help in getting spots for Little on every variety and talk show imaginable.

Little regularly did impressions of actors and politicians, augmenting likeness of voice with the mannerisms of those he impersonated. His most famous act was his impression of Richard Nixon, exaggerating the President's seemingly contrived smile and the raised arms with two fingers in the victory gesture. Nixonian declarations and demeanour provided Little with a wealth of lampooning opportunity until the Watergate scandal. After that, making fun of Nixon just did not seem to be the same anymore.

LUMBERJACK SONG

How did he get stuck in such a humdrum job? So wonders a dissatisfied Englishman who pines for testosterone-fuelled work in a manly setting. His aspiration is clear. "I wanted to be a lumberjack. Leaping from tree to tree as I float down the mighty rivers of British Columbia." He suddenly dons head-gear that resembles a cheap hunter's cap, complete with ear flaps. He sports a red-black plaid flannel shirt. He snuggles his fawning girlfriend and begins to sing "The Lumberjack Song." Staving off his English accent (somewhat unsuccessfully) he launches into the ridiculous ditty, backed by a cluster of forest-loving Mounties repeating every nonsensical line he sings. The lyrics get sillier—and sillier yet. By the end, using today's standards, they break every boundary of political correctness. But it is 1969. And it is a Monty Python skit. And no foreigners seem to be bothered to take a comedic swipe at the north country; it always seems to be Canadians poking fun at themselves. We Canucks should be honoured that an ensemble like the Python group took such an interest!

The Monty Python comedy troupe's TV program began on the British Broadcasting Corporation (BBC) in 1969 and was picked up by the CBC a year later. The Canadian broadcast allowed some American audiences living close to the border to see the quirky brand of humour that was so popular across the Atlantic. It was not until 1974 that *Monty Python's Flying Circus* was carried by the Public Broadcasting Service (PBS) in the United States. The troupe never reached the cult status there that they achieved amongst a good number of Canadian youths.

In 1975 the "Lumberjack Song" was released as an A-side single in the United Kingdom. The B-side was "The Spam Song." Former Beatle and Python fan George Harrison produced the record.

MUZZLING STEINBERG AND HIS PALS

Winnipeg-born David Steinberg attended a Jewish high school in Chicago and began his theological studies in that city. However, comedy was more his style and he joined the Chicago SCTV troupe before being noticed by Johnny Carson. He eventually appeared on the *Tonight Show* over 130 times, second in appearances only to Bob Hope.

In the late 1960s Steinberg's satirical sermons were a regular feature on *The Smothers Brothers* TV show. According to *TV Guide* Steinberg was "offbeat, racy, outrageous, and establishment-baiting." As such, he and his satirical sermons were a perfect fit for a comedy show that skirted the edges of what was then believed to be good taste. For those young and young-at-heart Canadians, *The Smothers Brothers* was an easy program to like.

Rob Reiner, later Michael in *All in the Family*, and Steve Martin were two of the writers. The dopey Pat Paulsen was a perennially unsuccessful presidential candidate. The musical segments featured a who's-who of the anti-establishment crowd—Joan Baez, Cream, the Who, the Doors, and Jefferson Airplane. The humour was topical and satirical.

Like so much of the youth-oriented entertainment industry in the late 1960s, the brother's fame was relatively brief, assisted by a well-publicized battle with representatives of the "establishment."

In an example of the supposed generation gap, the Smothers Brothers ran afoul of the CBS network executives. The bigwigs were particularly annoyed with the regularly appearing Canadian comedian. Borrowing from his theological background, Steinberg's satirical "sermons" generated a record number of letters of complaint. Itching for a scrap with the executives, Tom Smothers was impressed. The curmudgeonly censors were not. CBS refused to air a specific show due to a particularly "offensive" Steinberg routine. The Smothers Brothers fought back, railing against alleged censorship. CBS cancelled the show. As one network executive explained, "The Smothers Brothers were unwilling to accept the criteria of taste established by CBS."

The Smothers Brothers sued CBS for breach of contract. After four years of litigation, they won a 1973 settlement of $776,000 USD, the equivalent of roughly $5.1 million in 2023. They attempted a more sanitized variety show in 1975. However, in a remarkably short span of time the world had moved on. The appeal of their comedic style had waned and the comeback was unsuccessful

Steinberg meanwhile, was *hired* by CBS for a summer replacement show (1972). The comedian returned to Canada and headlined another one-year program with CTV in 1976. Many of the Canadian comedians on Toronto's *SCTV* program did double duty that year, appearing on the Steinberg show as well. In later years Steinberg became a sitcom producer, churning out episodes of *Seinfeld, Newhart, Mad About You,* and *Designing Women—see Chapter 8, SCTV Rocket Launch.*

OSSTIDCHO BOOSTS DESCHAMPS

By 1967 Yvon Deschamps was well known in Québec for his openly nation-alist (or separatist depending on one's viewpoint) monologues. The late 1960s *L'Osstidcho* was a musical-comedy revue fused with improvisation and seeming disorder that propelled him and fellow performer Robert Charlebois high up on the ladder of Québecois culture—a place they would remain throughout the 1970s.

Deschamps' comedic style at the time emphasized caustic humour. It was couched in spectacular naivete emanating from the low-income workers he portrayed. For instance, in the monologue of *Les unions, qu'ossa donne?* (unions, what are they good for?), the working class character praises his good boss, who of course is anything but. The message is diametrically opposed to what the character is stating.

Deschamps' monologues became even more sardonic throughout the 1970s. He was instrumental in inspiring a new generation of Québec come-dians that helped propel that province into a hotbed for stand-up comedy. In 1983, the Just for Laughs festival in Montreal began. By the second decade of the twenty-first-century it was the largest international comedy festival in the world—*see Chapter 2, Québec and Charlebois; Chapter 6, Playwright Tremblay in the Spotlight; Chapter 7, Lévesque 1976.*

PAPER-BAG COMIC

1970s hockey fans attending a game at Toronto's Maple Leaf Gardens were not the only ones putting a paper bag over their head. There was Dartmouth-born Murray Langston who was making a name for himself on the stand-up comedy circuit in the U.S. This included a few appearances on *Rowan and Martin's Laugh-In* and several years as a semi-regular on *The Sonny and Cher Show*. A failed night club enterprise and the abrupt halt of his paycheques from the cancellation of *Sonny and Cher* left Langston searching for work. Though he would later joke that he donned the paper bag because, "I had a really bad complexion and it was cheaper than Clearasil," he later revealed that he joined the daytime low-brow talent-show spoof, *The Gong Show,* due to a simple case of financial necessity. "If you were in the union and you appeared on *The Gong Show* you got a couple of hundred dollars," he explained in a later interview. Stand-up comics need to eat too.

No one was going to confuse *The Gong Show* with high-quality television. Previous daytime TV creations by Chuck Barris, such as *The Dating Game* and *The Newlywed Game*, were sophistication personified when compared to his new 1976 show. Apparently, Langston was so embarrassed at sinking to *The Gong Show* level, he stuck a paper bag on his head with cutouts for his eyes and nose. He was a hit and instantly became "The Unknown Comic." The routine stuck and became a regular feature on the show, competing in popularity with such classy acts as "Gene, Gene the Dancing Machine."

Langston could mine the paper bag routine for a while. He handed out pictures of himself, complete with a paper bag covering his head. He joked about getting a face lift by raising the bag off his head only to reveal another one underneath. He demonstrated ventriloquist skill using a paper bag "dummy," while easily forming the words from his mouth hidden behind the bag. Seemingly realizing that a schtick like his would not have a long shelf life he jumped into the late 1970s poster craze, mimicking the Burt Reynolds pose that had been run in *Playgirl.* The Unknown Poster featured Langston lounging back, paper bag in place over his head. A long wine bag covered his supposedly well-endowed private parts. In a later interview Langston claimed he never received any money for the poster. It will be left to the reader to speculate as to why.

The Gong Show ran from 1976 to 1978 with a few more years in syndication. By the early to mid-1980s "The Unknown Comic" routine had lost much of its lustre.

PRODUCER OF COMEDIC HEIGHTS

The mid to late 1970s was a take-off point for Canadian comedy. Edmonton-born Tommy Chong and American draft-resister Cheech Marin had perfected their stoner dude routine. *Second City Television* (SCTV) began and launched the careers of Eugene Levy and Catherine O'Hara (later to star in *Schitt's Creek*). Ottawa-born comedian Dan Ackroyd was a mainstay on *Saturday Night Live.*

In this mix, though usually behind the scenes, was Lorne Michaels. He had been a writer and broadcaster for CBC radio. He regarded Frank Shuster of the Wayne and Shuster duo as his mentor to such an extent he married

Shuster's daughter, Rosie. The couple left Canada in 1968 when Michaels joined the writing team of *Rowan and Martin's Laugh-In*.

In 1975 Michaels created *Saturday Night Live (SNL)*. Wife Rosie was one of the writers. The show had an initial cult following that soon became synonymous with hip satire. In the first season Michaels made a rare appearance on stage. In a deadpan voice he offered the deliberately paltry sum of $3,000 for the Beatles to reunite on the show. Perhaps Michaels knew that Paul McCartney and John Lennon were in New York at the time and may have been in the audience (they were not). Later George Harrison was a musical guest and joined in the fun, declaring with solemn pique that the offer was "chintzy." A straight-faced Michaels replied that the Beatles did not have to split the money evenly. "Give Ringo less," he said, tongue firmly placed in his cheek.

Beginning in October 2023, *Saturday Night Live* entered its 49th season. As of 2022 the show has received 305 Primetime Emmy Award nominations and won 93 times. Difficult to believe now, the show's initial audience ratings were relatively low. It was the show's creator, Michaels, who was able to convince the network executives that the mid-1970s audience was mainly comprised of the coveted "baby boomer" demographic. The boomers may have been viewing less television than they had in the past, but one show they did tune in to watch was *SNL*. They were in prime spending years too, always a bonus for advertisers. Given the show's popularity over the years, the network executives must have been pleased. So too were the advertisers.

Michaels has continued to be a main cog in *Saturday Night Live*. He also produced the series *Kids in the Hall* in 1988. He continues to be the Executive Producer of *The Tonight Show with Jimmy Fallon* and *Late Night with Seth Myer—see Chapter 8, SCTV Rocket Launch,* and *Yortuk as Classic Ackroyd*.

QUEEN LUBA OF THE FARCE

The Jest Society was a comedy troupe that began in Montreal in 1970 as a pun on Prime Minister Trudeau's statement about Canada needing to be "a just society." Ottawa-raised Luba Goy was a daughter of staunch Ukrainian nationalists who had immigrated to Canada in 1951. She joined the Jest Society in 1971 before the troupe eventually morphed into The Royal

Canadian Air Farce. Their comedy routines began airing on CBC radio in 1973 and television in 1977.

The comedic entourage parodied the politicians and newsmakers of the day. Throughout the 1970s, Goy was the sole female cast member. As such, she was the natural choice to lampoon such diverse figures as Yoko Ono, Elizabeth Taylor, and Barbara Streisand.

It seemed that Goy felt that Queen Elizabeth's family provided particularly memorable material. Her regal-spirited monologues were complete with the trappings of the sartorial splendour of Her Majesty. In one memorable Queen characterization, Goy stated, "I have never understood the public fascination with my family. We are just like any average family who live in a castle and have the collective IQ of a Yorkshire Pudding."

Ouch! Perhaps that is one of the benefits of comedy—being able to say what others are thinking—*see Chapter 8, Quintessential Broadfoot Barbs.*

QUINTESSENTIAL BROADFOOT BARBS

Another of the Royal Farce cast was David Broadfoot, the North Vancouver-born comedian who passed away in 2009. Broadfoot's take on "real" Canadian characters was his forte. A well-known depiction was of Royal Canadian Mounted Police (RCMP) officer Sergeant Renfrew. Despite his minimal competency at apprehending ne'er-do-wells, Renfrew was successful in gathering up promotions as easily as plucking pebbles from a beach. Another persona was Big Bobby Clobber, the dim-witted hockey player who had taken far too many hits to the head. He had a multi-sensory media system placed in his helmet. This allowed Clobber to listen to the play-by-play commentator and figure out who had the puck. Into this mix of clueless Canadian characters was David J. Broadfoot, a member of the National Apathetic Party, He was the MP for the barely-populated riding of Kicking Horse Pass and a man of questionable ethical standards. He once stated, "If an MP accepts a cash gratuity to do someone a favour, he should do it. Not to follow through would be dishonest!"

Despite his numerous comedic swipes at the RCMP via the inept Renfrew character, Broadfoot was made an honorary Sergeant Major of the force.

REAL LIFE PUMMELS HERMAN

British-born Jim Unger made Canada his home in 1968, eventually landing a job as a cartoonist for the *Mississauga Times*. Creating a cartoon character named "Attila the Bum," he sought a syndicated deal with a publisher. It was not uncommon at the time for Canadian musicians and artists to be first recognized outside the home country before being "discovered" by Canadians. This was the case with Unger. The *Toronto Star* rebuffed his offer. In hindsight this was not a good decision. In a few short years, the newly-named Herman cartoon character was being read by an estimated 40 million readers in over 600 newspapers in 25 countries. It was the Kansas City-based Universal Press Syndicate that signed Unger to a 10-year contract in 1974, only insisting that the title of the cartoon be changed. Herman, the downtrodden everyman, was born.

The saggy characters with oaf-like mentality, big noses, and sprigs of hair took on life as it came—and lost more-often-than-not. The henpecked husband Herman with the unattractive, unskilled, unmotivated wife inclined to incessant nagging speaks of a brand of humour from a bygone era. Yet according to Unger, Herman's exposure to ridicule made him universally appealing. Perhaps the trials and tribulations of the downtrodden everyman gave a boost of much-needed positive self-esteem to the reader. Pretty much everyone with close-to-average intelligence and looks stacked up pretty well against the hapless Herman.

According to a *Globe and Mail* article, Canada's high taxes, and what he termed creeping leftism, led Unger to move to the Bahamas (much like fellow Canadian writer Arthur Hailey). He maintained a home in Saanich on Vancouver Island and passed away there in 2012.

SCTV ROCKET LAUNCH

It was as if an eggshell had been broken and a batch of comedy hatchlings emerged. The Second City Stage Troupe in Toronto was an offshoot of the Chicago show (hence the second-city moniker describing Chicago's perennial rank to New York). John Candy and Catherine O'Hara became members of *Second City Television (SCTV)* for its inaugural season in 1976. Joining them were fellow Canadians, Dave Thomas, and Eugene Levy. These four Canucks, along with Americans Joe Flaherty, Harold Ramis, and Andrea Martin were the initial cast members. (Martin had been in Toronto since 1970 and after 47 years in the country opted for Canadian citizenship in 2017). Canadians Martin Short and Rick Moranis joined the show in subsequent years.

Mimicking a television network and the range of programs it aired, *SCTV* provided innovative and zany sketch comedy, akin to a Canadian version of Britain's Monty Python troupe. After the first episode, Margaret Daly of the *Toronto Star* noted, "Global TV may have just pulled off the comedy coup of the season. The concept is as clever as the loony company members."

SCTV went through numerous cast changes as many of the stars, including the main Canadian players, went on to successful movie careers. Members, such as John Candy, Martin Short, and Rick Moranis would join Dan Ackroyd (and later Mike Myers, Michael J. Fox, and Jim Carrey), as a troupe of Canadian men that were leaders in English-language film comedy in North America for the next dozen years—*see Chapter 8; Muzzling Steinberg and His Pals, Producer of Comedic Heights,* and *Two Minutes with Bob and Doug.*

STONER DUDES

Spending time in and around the west coast music scene in the late 1960s was former prairie-boy Tommie Chong and American draft-resister Cheech Marin. The duo began to ride the counterculture tsunami with their stoner comedy routine first introduced in Vancouver bars. Having an entertainment niche is good for business when you are one of the few participants. Cheech and Chong became the most well-known of a small group of reefer-addicted comedy acts. The humour may have been juvenile and one-dimensional; but it was topical, at least to pot-smoking adolescents and young adults. Cheech and Chong's audience was not middle-aged accountants and suburban soccer moms. They were established enough to win a Grammy Award for the Best Comedy Album in 1973 with *Los Cochinos*. Smokin' and tokin' their way through the 1970s, their first full length movie was *Up in Smoke* in 1978.

In the mid-1980s Cheech and Chong attempted an unsuccessful departure from stoner comedy before dissolving the partnership in 1985 to concentrate on solo careers. In 2018 Mr. Chong was planning to return to Canada to celebrate the legalization of cannabis. But as the *Toronto Star* reported, in true stoner-style, "He couldn't find his passport."

TWO MINUTES WITH BOB AND DOUG

It was a request (from the network's perspective) or demand (from the actor's viewpoint), for an additional few minutes of specific Canadian content on *SCTV*. It inadvertently sparked the creation of the most successful comedy sketch routine in the program's history—the Great White North segment that started in 1980. Originally intended as a simple throw-away to meet the bureaucratic requirement, the spot became a huge hit, ironically sending a message to the world about Canadians that did not mesh with any network or government mandate. Rick Moranis and Dave Thomas portrayed two "hosers" intent on spending most of their time scarfing down copious quantities of back-bacon and emptying unending bottles of Canadian beer. In the background was a map of Canada, devoid of inscriptions and place names and enveloped with a seemingly deep blanket of snow, no matter the time of the year. Dressed in toques and checked flannel outerwear, the dim-witted duo became icons of the Canadian culture they parodied. Until the "hosers" began their ramblings, many Canadians may not have realized the frequency with which they stuck "eh" onto spoken phrases.

As for network executives who had asked for more time to showcase Canadian content—sometimes it is better to not ask the question if one does not know what the answer will be—*see Chapter 8, SCTV Rocket Launch.*

YORTUK AS CLASSIC ACKROYD

Yortuk was one half of the Yortuk and Elwood combo that was featured on *Saturday Night Live.* While the duo may sound like an ambulance-chasing law firm on the wrong side of town, instead it showcased the wide-ranging comedic talent of Dan Ackroyd, born and raised in Ottawa. After spending time on the CBC children's television series *Coming Up Rosie,* Ackroyd signed on as a writer on the new U.S. comedy sketch show *Saturday Night Live.* Lest readers think that such gigs are paved with gold, Ackroyd's initial writing salary was $278 per week, not a particularly massive haul of money, even by 1975 standards. Soon Ackroyd was part of the cast. Soon after that he was a star. By the 1980s he was headlining major motion pictures. In those later years it would be reasonable to believe that Ackroyd was hauling in more than $278 before his coffee break on Monday morning.

A classic Ackroyd character on *SNL* was as one of the Festrunk brothers (Yortuk). Along with Steve Martin, the socially inept, culturally clueless duo from Eastern Europe frequented bars and discos searching for "foxy" American women. Dressed in outrageous attire they erroneously believed to be hip, the pair inevitably struck out with the ladies. Given that they self-described as "two wild and crazy guys" there was always next week when the fruitless hunt would commence yet again.

Ackroyd worked just as well with another partner in an entirely different role. His love of blues music influenced fellow *SNL* cast member John Belushi. The two formed The Blues Brothers, Ackroyd as Elwood and Belushi as Jake. They debuted on *Saturday Night Live* and later headlined the 1980 movie blockbuster, *The Blues Brothers*.

After 1980, Ackroyd starred in films such as *Trading Places, Ghostbusters,* and *Driving Miss Daisy,* the latter film for which he was nominated for an Academy Award for Best Supporting Actor.

9

SPORTS STORIES

During the 60–80 era, sports performances by Canadians ranged from unexpected victories to disappointing defeat. In hockey the trajectory was decidedly downhill, from a world-championship crown for the Trail Smoke Eaters squad in 1961 to Canadian professionals snatching a last-minute victory in the 1972 Summit Series. After winning the inaugural Canada Cup in 1976, Canadian NHLers (with three Swedes) lost 6–0 to the Soviets in the Challenge Cup in 1979. Two years later, the agony of defeat intensified. Canada was pummelled 8–1 by the Soviets in the final game of the Canada Cup.

Success in other sports was sporadic, though with some highlight performances (Harry Jerome, Nancy Greene, Sandy Hawley, Ferguson Jenkins). The Canadian Football league had its golden era, while professional soccer and lacrosse stumbled out of the starting gate.

The upward directional change toward success in the Olympics began slowly. For much of the 60–80 era Canadian athletes did not fare well. It seemed that Canadians were content with a good effort as opposed to a commitment to winning. But a foundation was being laid. Later, in a slow but steady pace, results began to change. Canadians began to count wins as opposed to near misses. Eventually, after the turn of the millennium, the Canadian transition was complete—from nicely-behaved non-medallists to those meeting with success through the current official push to "own the podium."

A COUNTRY-WIDE FOOTBALL LEAGUE

The field is wider and longer; the ball fatter. There are 12 players on the field rather than 11. The team has only three down to make ten yards, not four. Teams in the Canadian Football League (CFL) play a notably different version of football than what is found in the United States.

The CFL was formed in 1958. The championship Grey Cup game had been contested since 1909 but it was not until 1921 that western teams competed for the title. For most years thereafter, the champion of the Interprovincial Rugby Football Union met their counterpart from the Western Interprovincial Football Union and played for the Grey Cup. The eastern teams tended to dominate the matches until the mid-1950s when the Edmonton Eskimos; led by Jackie Parker, Johnny Bright, and Canadian Normie Kwong, won three straight Grey Cups against the Sam Etcheverry-led Montreal Alouettes.

Limited interlocking play between the newly-named Western and Eastern Conferences did not start until 1961 when Trans-Canada Airlines was making it easier to traverse the country. It was one thing to travel by train from Calgary to Toronto to play in a Grey Cup championship game—quite another to make that trip for one regular season match. It was not until 1974 that the eastern team's schedules were increased to 16 games to match that in the west.

The CFL has always had a rule limiting the number of non-Canadian players. Despite various changes over the years the intent of the import rule remained the same—to reserve spots on team rosters for Canadians and prevent the league from being swamped by American players. That the Canadian players have tended to be assigned to the less-skilled positions has never been addressed.

Always on the hunt for revenue, on ten occasions Canadian teams played American squads in exhibition games. Five of those occurred shortly after the formation of the CFL. They were held mid-season for CFL teams and as pre-season exhibition games for the American sides. In 1960 the Pittsburgh Steelers defeated the Toronto Argonauts 43–16. A year later the Argos lost again; this time 36–7 to the St. Louis Cardinals. The Montreal Alouettes went down to defeat against the Chicago Bears 34–16. Defending the CFL honour, the Hamilton Tiger Cats bested the-then American Football League's (AFL) Buffalo Bills 38–21 in that same year.

The games were played in Canada and were well-attended. Adding to the mystique was the change in rules at half-time. One half of the game was played with American rules, the other with those of the CFL. Given that the American teams won most of the contests, the CFL's three downs, larger ball, wider field, and one extra player did not seem to be a significant hindrance— *see Chapter 9, Saskatchewan's Rider Pride.*

BUT WE WANT GOLD!

Canadians did not have much opportunity to gloat about their country's medallists at the Summer Olympics in the 60-80 era. In the five Games held from 1960 to 1976 (Canada boycotted the 1980 event) Canadians won *two* gold medals. The United States won 182. Sweden and Australia, each with roughly half Canada's population at the time, won 13 and 27 gold medals respectively. The medal tally in Winter Olympics was almost as abysmally low. In the six Winter Olympics held during the 60–80 era Canada won a grand total of five gold medals (none of them in ice hockey). Perhaps that explains the ridiculously high expectations for a gold medal when the occasional Canadian was favoured to win—and the equally absurd level of criticism when that did not happen.

In the early 1960s Harry Jerome was one of the world's greatest sprinters. He had equalled the world record in the 100 metres in 1960 and was favoured to win a gold medal at the 1960 Olympic Games in Rome. In the semi-finals Jerome was forced to pull up due to a hamstring injury. The media jackals began to bray. Jerome was labelled a "quitter" who "couldn't handle the pressure." Jerome fired off a verbal volley in response. Perhaps because he was a black man, the media types were even more inflamed at the audacity.

The next year Jerome tied the world record in the 100-yard sprint. At the 1962 Commonwealth Games he tore the quadriceps in his left leg, a significant and debilitating injury. The *Vancouver Sun* issued a "Jerome Folds Again" headline. Only after many of the Canadian officials and track teammates came out in support of the sprinter did several media outlets alter their commentary. After a serious operation, Jerome returned to win a bronze medal at the 1964 Olympic Games. He followed that up with a gold medal at the Commonwealth Games two years later. There is a three-metre statue commemorating Jerome that is placed along Vancouver's Stanley Park seawall.

While Jerome was winning in 1966, 15-year-old Canadian Elaine Tanner was scorching the Commonwealth Games pool. Dubbed "Mighty Mouse," world record holder Tanner won four gold and three silver medals. She was named Canada's Best Athlete for 1966. Dominant wins the following year put her in the driver's seat for a gold medal at the 1968 Olympic Games in Mexico City. In her specialty she came within a millimetre of victory. The silver medal was a crushing disappointment. As soon as the race was over, the media hawks barraged her with the same question of "why didn't you win?" asked a dozen different ways. One newspaper summarized the disappointment with a single headline, "Tanner Loses Gold." She was consoled by the one person who truly understood what she was going through—Harry Jerome.

Despite adding another individual Olympic silver and a relay bronze, Tanner could not erase the failure of the unmet expectations of the media and public. Starting shortly afterward she led a decades-long vagabond existence, being marginally employed in low-paying jobs. Her marriage ended; her children lived with her ex-husband. She was consumed by emotional fragility, eating disorders, and depression.

Tanner has since remarried, recovered, and reconnected with her children. For several years she has been an advocate for increasing support levels for those with mental health issues—*see Chapter 9, Setting a Uniquely High Bar.*

FAST HORSES WITH NORTHERN BLOOD

In 1964, Northern Dancer was the first Canadian-bred horse to win the Kentucky Derby. To make matters even more interesting, the horse won the second leg of America's famed Triple Crown by winning the Preakness that same year. A win in the third race, the Belmont Stakes, would have made the horse from Canada the first U.S. Triple Crown winner since Citation in 1948. Alas, Northern Dancer finished third. Though slightly injured, Northern Dancer won its last race—the 1964 Queen's Plate, the first leg of the Canadian Triple Crown (the Prince of Wales Stakes and the Breeders' Stakes being the other high-profile races).

Proving that it was just as proficient at a roll in the hay as running around a racetrack, Northern Dancer was put out to stud in 1965. It sired Nijinsky, a horse that won the prestigious English Triple Crown in 1970. Since many judges ruled out the winners of three key races during World War I, Nijinsky was considered only the third horse after 1900 to win the English Triple Crown. It was also the last horse to accomplish the feat, making Northern Dancer famous again, this time as a stud.

IRON-JAW CHUVALO

Muhammad Ali had a loquacious start, verbally sparring with straight-man interviewer Howard Cosell in the early to mid-1960s. Lines such as: "I'm the greatest, I said that even before I knew I was. I'm so mean I make medicine sick;" or, "My only fault is that I don't realize how great I really am" were blabbered by Ali. A solemn-faced Cosell attempted to keep the interview on-track as Ali built his brand.

Ali was as nimble on his feet as he was with his mouth. Few people wanted to climb into the ring with him in the 1960s. In his first 23 professional fights most of his opponents were dispatched by knockout or technical knockout long before the 15 rounds were completed. Up until 1966 former world champion Floyd Patterson had lasted the longest, making it to the 12th round before succumbing.

In March 1966 world champion Ali met the Canadian champion George Chuvalo in Maple Leaf Gardens. Chuvalo had never been knocked to the canvas floor. That streak would continue. Iron-Jaw Chuvalo lasted a full 15 rounds against Ali, taking a terrible beating much of the time but surviving enough for the referee to allow him to continue the fight. Try as he might, Ali could not knock the Canadian champ to the mat. Until Ali lost the heavyweight crown to Joe Frasier in 1971, only Ernie Terrell in 1967 matched Chuvalo's feat of staying in the ring for 15 rounds with the champion. Ali later said that Chuvalo was "the toughest guy I ever fought."

JACKSON – THE CANADIAN QB

Until the sudden 2022 arrival of the BC Lions' Nathan Rourke, there have been very few Canadians playing the quarterback (QB) position in the CFL—and none that have made any impact. Except Russ Jackson.

Those who came of age in the 60–80 period will remember Jackson as the Ottawa Rough Riders' quarterback throughout the 1960s. He was a strong leader, a deft passer, and an especially good runner for a quarterback. Jim Trimble, the former coach of the Philadelphia Eagles and Montreal Alouettes said that Jackson "could play anywhere in the NFL."

The Canadian QB won three Grey Cups. He was the Most Outstanding Player in the league, American or Canadian, three times. He was named Canada's Best Athlete in 1969, being the only football player to win the award for 44 years until Jon Cornish did so in 2013. He is ranked #8 on the list of the greatest CFL players, the only Canadian to crack the top ten. Only one other Canadian in the 60–80 era was selected as the league's Most Outstanding Player—Tony Gabriel the Ottawa tight-end in 1978 (Gabriel also won the top Canadian award in 1974, 1976, and 1977). Besides Jackson and Gabriel, only two other Canadians of the 60–80 era won the Most Outstanding Canadian award more than once—Terry Evanshen, with Calgary and Montreal, and Jim Young with the BC Lions.

It was not unusual for CFL players of the 60–80 era to have a second job. Jackson was a high school Math teacher from 1959 to 1966. After retiring from football in 1969, he resumed his education career and became a principal of a high school in 1973.

JENKINS AND THE BLACK ACES

Ferguson Jenkins was born in Chatham, Ontario. His father was from Barbados and his mother was a descendent of American slaves who had travelled north via the Underground Railroad. Jenkins began his baseball career in the mid-1960s when the number of black players in the major leagues was increasing. Players such as Frank Robinson, Willie Mays, and Hank Aaron were amongst the best in the game. Few however, were pitchers. As with football's black quarterbacks, black pitchers were frequently converted into position players. There were even fewer Canadians. Only eight Canucks were on active rosters in the-then twenty-team Major Leagues of approximately 500 players. Being black, a pitcher, and a Canadian was a triple hurdle that certainly made Jenkins a rarity in major league baseball at the time. But it was his ability on the mound that made him a stand-out.

Jenkins' best seasons were with the Chicago Cubs. It was with that team that he won the National League's Cy Young Award as the best pitcher in 1971, the first Canadian player to do so (only one other Canadian has won that award—Éric Gagné in 2003). Jenkins enjoyed seven seasons of 20 wins or more (including six in a row), and was the first Canadian inducted into baseball's Hall of Fame in 1991 (Larry Walker followed in 2020). He is a member of the so-called Black Aces, the black pitchers who won 20 games in a season, being only the fifth to do so (after Don Newcombe, Sam Jones, Mudcat Grant, and Bob Gibson).

In his home country Jenkins won the award as Canada's top athlete in 1974. His image can be found on a Canadian stamp since 2011 when it was issued to commemorate Black History Month. At the time, Jenkins was travelling throughout Canada raising awareness of black history initiatives.

KING KONG MOSCA

Angelo Mosca played only a brief time in Ottawa and Montreal. It was his years with the Hamilton Tiger Cats from 1962 to 1972 that cemented his reputation as a tough customer on the football field. Perhaps he was preparing for his future wrestling career when he flew missile-like across, or onto (depending on one's point of view) star BC Lions player Willie Fleming during the 1963 Grey Cup game at Empire Stadium in Vancouver. Piling onto a player in a football game is hardly a basis for notoriety. But it is when the grounded player is the opposition's best player and is lying well over the sidelines, out-of-bounds. There was no penalty called on the play.

The burly Mosca provided an unusual response to the resultant debate about whether the hit was clean or not. "I created an image and everyone thinks I'm dirty. There's no such thing as a dirty play unless you're kicking people in the face."

Appearing in nine Grey Cup games, Mosca was on the winning side five times. After retiring from playing football, he continued to live in the Hamilton area. He had wrestled in the off-season, so when he hung up his pads he donned a pair of tights. He grappled full-time against opponents in major arenas, most often as a bad-boy with the moniker King Kong Mosca.

Decades later, a luncheon in Vancouver turned into a mini-brawl between two men in their seventies. Mosca and Joe Kapp, the BC Lions quarterback during the Willie Fleming incident, punched and tussled with each other. The well-publicized affair may have reflected true animosity between the two old men, or may have been a staged publicity event that was perfect for today's attention-grabbing postings found on YouTube.

MAKE WAY FOR ORR

In the 1950s and 1960s a top puck-handling defenceman like Doug Harvey of the Montreal Canadiens or Pierre Pilote of the Chicago Black Hawks would score between 50 and 60 points a season (Harvey's best was 50 points in 70 games; Pilote's was 59 in 68 games).

Then came Parry Sound native, Bobby Orr.

The Boston Bruins signed Orr to a C form in 1962 when he was in his early teens. This linked the young phenom to their team. The Bruins paid the family $10,000 (equivalent to about $95,500 in 2023) and provided a new car. Three other teams were interested in Orr—Toronto, Montreal, and Detroit. But those three were top-level teams at the time. Boston was a perennial bottom-feeder. The teenage Orr saw the Bruins as a team of the future.

Beginning in 1969–1970, Orr scored over 100 points in six-straight seasons. Unlike the plodding defencemen of days past, Orr was a fast and fluid skater, willing to join, or even lead the forwards on the attack. He won the scoring title twice. His 139 points in the 1970–1971 season remains the single-season record for most points by a defenceman, though the term rover may better describe the position he played.

Knee injuries prevented Orr from playing in the 1972 Summit Series against the Soviet Union. However, after signing with the Chicago Black Hawks and being hampered by new injuries, he was selected as the Most

Valuable Player (MVP) in the 1976 Canada Cup tournament. According to teammate Darryl Sittler, "Orr was better on one leg than anybody else was on two."

Ten years of taking numerous hits while carrying the puck all over the ice on the small-sized Boston Garden ice probably contributed to Orr's relatively short career. He played limited portions of three seasons in Chicago. After over a dozen surgeries on his left knee, he retired in 1978, playing in only 36 games over his last four seasons.

NOT A BEAUTIFUL START

Today there are three well-established Canadian markets in Major league Soccer (Vancouver Whitecaps, Toronto FC, and CF Montreal). There is a Canadian Professional League. The national women's team won the gold medal at the 2021 Olympics in Tokyo. The men's team participated in the 2022 World Cup and boasts some bona fide young stars. Soccer in Canada today is on the upswing.

It has not always been this way. The story of the professional game in Canada in the 60–80 period is one of general doom and gloom, punctuated with glimmers of hope and promise. It may be known worldwide as the beautiful game, but the start of professional soccer in North America bordered on ugly.

Investors had been impressed with the North American TV audience for the 1966 World Cup final. Of course, the soccer they were to eventually offer in North America was a far cry from England vs. West Germany in front of 100,000 spectators at London's Wembley Stadium.

In 1967 there were two rival leagues in North America. The Vancouver Royals and Toronto City played in a league that somehow managed the staggering level of incompetence of failing to have player contracts signed before the season started. Entire teams (or at least their reserve squads) were transported from the U.K. The Royals were England's Sunderland. Toronto City was Scotland's Hibernia. The Toronto Falcons played in the rival league.

In 1968 the two leagues merged and formed the North American Soccer League (NASL). The Falcons and Royals played for one season and then folded. Toronto was back in the fold in 1971 as the Toronto Metros. Fifty percent of the franchise was purchased by a long-time local team, Toronto Croatia in 1975. The team had an unwieldly name, the Toronto Metros-Croatia. It was thankfully renamed the Toronto Blizzard when the franchise was sold again in 1978. You just cannot make this stuff up!

At least in Vancouver a person could keep track of the team's name. The Vancouver Whitecaps began in the 1974 season and drew respectable crowds, winning the 1979 Soccer Bowl over the Tampa Bay Rowdies.

The NASL owners thought big. You need to spend money to make money—right? Led by the New York Cosmos, franchises spent big dollars on big-name players who were past their prime; in some cases, well past their prime. The strategy worked for a short time as attendance increased. Rules were altered, including time-outs for commercials to make the game more TV (advertising) friendly. But with the average attendance across the league never reaching the 15,000 mark, and with network TV contracts coming and going, the writing was on the wall. In 1984, the first attempt at a high-level professional version of the beautiful game in North America came to a not-so-pretty end when the NASL ceased operation.

POSTING VICTORIES ON THE LADIES' TOUR

Oakville's Sandra Post became the first Canadian to join the women's profes-sional tour in 1968. In fact, from an American perspective, she was the first foreigner to join the tour that today seems dominated by non-Americans, particularly young women from South Korea.

Post made quite a splash when she dived into the Ladies' Professional Golf Association (LPGA) pool. In the same year she joined the tour she became the youngest golfer to win the LPGA championship event, one of the game's major tournaments. It was just after her twentieth birthday when Post defeated the well-established Kathy Whitworth in a playoff. Though today's teens regularly defeat their older rivals, Post's youngest-ever record survived for almost 40 years and was finally broken in 2007. After her LPGA win, it would be another 48 years before another Canadian woman would be victo-rious at a major tournament when Brooke Henderson won in 2016.

Post's best season on the tour was 1979 when she finished second on the LPGA money list. In that year she was named Canada's best athlete. More importantly she helped pave the way for the next generation of Canadian women who would grapple with the emotional anguish and mental frustration inherent in golf—a challenge faced by weekend hackers and touring professionals alike.

ROLL CALL OF BEST ATHLETES

During the 60–80 era it is logical to assume that high profile hockey players would often be the first choice on the ballot for Canada's Athlete of the Year. As if to demonstrate that the Great White North produced more sports legends than just gap-toothed hockey players, the selectors chose only four puck chasers over the 60–80 span—Bobby Orr in 1970, Phil Esposito in 1972, Bobby Clarke in 1975, and Guy Lafleur in 1977. Hockey players who never won the award included perennial 50-goal-scorer Bobby Hull, frequent Stanley Cup winner Jean Beliveau, and the never-aging Gordie Howe.

In the 21 years from 1960 to 1980 inclusive only two athletes won the award twice. The first double winner (1967 and 1968) was Rossland BC alpine skier, Nancy Greene. She won the first yearly World Cup Ski Championship in 1967, ending the European domination of the sport. The aggressive skiing style that gave her the nickname "Tiger" worked again in 1968 when she won the World Cup and added a gold and silver medal at the Olympics.

In retirement Greene was influential in the development of the Whistler ski resort, bringing her "Tiger" style from the slopes to the boardrooms of upscale developers. Though the Whistler ski hill had opened in 1966 it was not until the late 1970s when the current townsite was developed, promoted by Greene and her husband Al Raine. The new village lay four kilometres north of the Alta Lake settlement, built over an area that had been that community's garbage dump. Greene then turned to politics and publicly supported the Reform Party in the 1990s. She was appointed to the Canadian Senate as a Conservative in 2009 and retired from that position at 75 years of age.

Jockey Sandy Hawley also won twice as Canada's Best Athlete in the 60–80 span (1973 and 1976). In the 1970s Hawley won 10 Canadian Triple Crown races—The Queen's Plate, The Prince of Wales Stakes, and The Breeders' Stakes. In 1973 he won 515 races, eclipsing Bill Shoemaker's previous record of 485. In the next year Hawley broke the money-winning record for one season. When racing in California, Hawley found a way to stay in touch with his second favourite sport of ice hockey by working as a penalty time-keeper for Los Angeles Kings games,

Over a long career Hawley rode a horse's back in an official race 31,435 times, parading to the victory circle on 6,450 occasions. This meant that there was already an approximate 20 percent chance that Hawley's horse would win before horse quality, track conditions, tarot cards, or grandpa's advice were considered when determining a wager. A man of stamina, on two occasions Hawley won seven races in one day—on two others, he won six times; feats that anyone who has spent any time riding a horse can only marvel at.

The Ontario Sports Hall of Fame presents the Sandy Hawley Award each year to an athlete who has demonstrated dedication to the community.

It is time for another quiz and you know it is a tough one when even the directions are complex. Firstly, leave out the four hockey players named above who won in 1970, 1972, 1975, and 1977. Secondly, leave out the two athletes also named above (Greene and Hawley) who combined to win in 1967, 1968, 1973, and 1976. Lastly, leave out the athletes already mentioned in earlier entries of this chapter who won the award: Tanner 1966, Jackson 1969, Jenkins 1974, and Post 1979. This leaves several years in which you, the reader, has not been given the answer. So, the task is to name the athlete who won the award as Canada's best athlete in those other years of the 60-80 era. This is so tough that, in addition to the year, the sport and the gender of the winner are provided as follows: 1960 Skiing (female); 1961 Track and Field (male); 1962 Figure Skating (male); 1963 Track and Field (male); 1964 Rowing (2 males); 1965 Figure Skating (female); 1971 Harness Racing (male); 1978 Skiing and Swimming (2 males); 1980 Charity Run (male). The answers are provided in Appendix C. Good luck! Even a sports nut will need it!

SASKATCHEWAN'S RIDER PRIDE

Branding is everything in contemporary marketing. Corporations have always built brands, spurred on by the billions of dollars spent on advertising. Today, social media has led to personal branding. Any individual can trumpet their wares, spread their opinions, boast about their influence, and build a brand. Canadian sports teams were surprisingly slow on the uptake. Then some owners realized that they could make a truckload of money on jerseys, hats, T-shirts, and the like. Though winning on the field or the ice helped, it was not essential, especially if a brand had been built that could withstand less-than-optimum competitive performance.

The Saskatchewan Roughriders built their "Rider Pride" during the 1960s and 1970s and it has continued unabated since. When operating in a small market, underdog status can help build the brand. Legendary Roughrider receiver Hugh Campbell ("Gluey Hughy") joined the team in 1963. Upon visiting the home stadium of Taylor Field, he noted that, "It looked like a farmer had built it ... and half the dressing room was dirt floor." At the time, Taylor Field held 15,365 spectators, less than half the capacity of Vancouver's relatively new Empire Stadium, home of the BC Lions. The stadium's capacity was increased to 19,195 in 1966, the same year the 'Riders won their first Grey Cup.

Taylor Field was tough on the players. It was no picnic for the fans either. The blustery fall and early-winter winds often called for a little alcoholic sustenance to be covertly sipped while shivering in the stands. In the 1970s, ramps on the West side of the stadium meant fans had to trudge up the equivalent of 17 or more stories to reach their seats. Yet when the Taylor Field stands were finally torn down to make way for the new Mosaic Stadium, fans rushed to buy auctioned seats and even portions of the turf. Anyone who braved the elements to watch a Roughriders game in the 1960s and 1970s will say there was no better place in Canada to watch a football game.

As the brand was being built, it helped that the 'Riders were good—but not great. After winning the Grey Cup in 1966 the team made it to the Western Championship game an astonishing ten consecutive times. They lost that game 6 times (1968, 1970, 1971, 1973, 1974, and 1975). On the four occasions when the team did manage to win the Western final and advance to the Grey Cup game, they lost every time (1967, 1969, 1972, and 1976)—*see Chapter 9, A Country-Wide Football League.*

SETTING A UNIQUELY HIGH BAR

Sixteen-year-old Debbie Brill was the first North American woman to clear six feet (the measurement used in the day) in woman's high jump. What is more, Brill leapt over the bar *backward* which the purists believed to be bizarre at best. Brill's decision to tackle high jump competitions using the unorthodox approach was done independently of Dick Fosbury, the American high-jumper known for the "Fosbury Flop." It, and the "Brill Bend," became the standard style for high jumping that has continued to this day.

After winning a gold medal at the 1970 Commonwealth and 1971 Pan American Games, the unconventional Brill quit jumping five months before the 1972 Munich Olympics. She reconsidered and competed, finishing eighth and disappointing the Canadian media-hawks who had expected better. She then campaigned to have the Games halted because of the massacre of 11 Israeli athletes. Disheartened by the Olympic experience, Brill quit the sport again. She stuck her thumb out and hit the road hitchhiking, as many of those coming of age did in the early 1970s. Some Canadian sportswriters expected an athlete to behave more "appropriately" and voiced less-than-complimentary opinions about Brill in various newspaper columns.

Returning to competition at the 1976 Montreal Olympics, Brill failed to clear the opening height which, for her, was set ridiculously low. Her seemingly casual, chuckling response to the failure led some sports commentators, so hungry for Canadian success, to be critical of her attitude. Bob Pickett of CBC Radio said, "Perhaps even if you have to fake it, you have to shed a few tears." Whether the media would have been so critical of a male athlete who displayed such an unconventional approach to sporting competition is a good question.

By 1979 Brill was ranked the best female high jumper in the world and a favourite for a gold medal at the 1980 Olympics in Moscow. Her hopes were dashed when Canada joined other western nations in boycotting the event due to the Soviet invasion of Afghanistan.

In 2014 Brill reflected on her Olympic experience, putting a refreshing perspective on the event, particularly when the stresses and scandals impacting young athletes are often in today's news. "You get to the Olympics and all the enjoyment you may have had in the sport is not very evident there. You're stuck there with thousands of incredibly stressed human beings."

Brill is a member of the Canadian Olympic Hall of Fame and the Order of Canada. Yet, despite these honours: including holding the Canadian women's high jump record for decades, winning multiple medals in international competitions, and creating a totally new method of approaching her sport, Debbie Brill is not a member of Canada's Sports Hall of Fame—*see Chapter 9, But We Want Gold!*

THE OTHER NATIONAL SPORT

What is Canada's official national sport—ice hockey or lacrosse? In an example of a typical Canadian compromise the answer is both.

Each sport laid claim to being the official one. Why Canada needed to declare a national sport is a good question, But the issue must have been important to some parliamentarians. In 1994 the National Sports Act of Canada was passed. Ice hockey was declared Canada's official winter sport—lacrosse the official summer sport.

In 2023 the National Lacrosse League (NLL) has five teams based in Canada: the Vancouver Warriors, the Calgary Roughnecks, the Saskatchewan (Saskatoon) Rush, the Toronto Rock, and the Halifax Thunderbirds. The season begins in the *winter* throwing a bit of a wrench into the official summer sport status.

Lacrosse was an Indigenous game with variations in name; examples being *baggataway* in Ojibwe and *tewaarathon* in Mohawk. Sometimes played on fields a kilometre in length and lasting several days, lacrosse (so named by Europeans linking it to a Bishop's crosier or *crosse, en francais)* was part athletic competition, part spiritual activity, and part conflict resolution amongst Indigenous nations.

The men's and women's versions of the modern field lacrosse game is a much more structured and milder version of those Indigenous marathons.

Canada, and several Indigenous teams whose membership straddles the Canada-U.S. border, have been very successful in international competitions.

It is the box version of lacrosse that has had fits and starts of popularity in Canada. It was originally developed as an activity to fill empty hockey arenas in the summer, with the Mann Cup being the men's national trophy. National may be stretching the point. For over 100 years the east-west competition has only been between a team from Ontario and one from BC.

The first attempt to professionalize box lacrosse was in the 60–80 era with a six-team operation. The league lasted two years (1974 and 1975) with three Canadian teams: the Montreal Québecois, the Toronto Tomahawks (1974 only), and the Québec Caribous (1975 only). The latter team celebrated its only season by defeating Montreal for the championship.

With fast action, plenty of goals, a few fights, and apparent permission to board, slash, and cross-check opponents, it is surprising that professional box lacrosse has not come closer to rivalling hockey in popularity. Perhaps NHL hockey's sky-high ticket prices will send those fans seeking an evening watching a little organized violence to a professional lacrosse game instead.

TOP LEAFS TOSSED ASIDE

To paraphrase Dickens, it was the best of time and the worst of times for the Leafs Nation in the 60–80 era. The team won four Stanley Cups in the 1960s; built around aged Johnny Bower in goal, hard-rock Tim Horton on defence, goal-scorer Frank Mahavolich, and the smooth-skating centre, Dave Keon.

Harold Ballard had been a senior executive with the organization throughout the 1960s and became majority owner of the team during the 1971–1972 season. Shortly after, Ballard was charged with 49 counts of fraud, theft, and tax evasion. He was eventually convicted on 47 of them, a 96 percent conviction rate that would please any prosecutor. Ballard only served a portion of his sentence and most of that was in a minimum-security institution. When he was released from the "slammer" he took control of the team. In the early 1970s the Leafs were mediocre at best. By the mid to late 1970s they were better on the ice but were a media circus off it. The blustery Ballard acted as the ringmaster.

The epitome of a hands-on owner, in mid-decade Ballard decided to change the team's leadership to a new cadre of stars led by Darryl Sittler. He let it be known that Dave Keon, who had been with the team for 15 years and was the only star remaining from the 1960s championship squads, was not wanted. He told Keon he could make his own deal with another NHL team. But Ballard retained Keon's NHL rights and set the compensation bar so high that other teams balked at signing the centre. Keon's only option was to play in the rival WHA, spending most of his time there with the New England Whalers. He came back in the NHL as a Whaler when that team joined the league in 1979.

Sittler was the new captain and star. He was also active in the NHL Players' Association (NHLPA). No friend of union malcontents, Ballard wanted to trade yet another captain despite, or perhaps because of, Sittler's increasing prominence. However, Sittler had a no-trade clause that would cost Ballard $500,000 to waive. Being cheap, Ballard would not pay. Being canny, he found another way to punish Sittler. He was ably assisted by his newly hired retread general manager Punch Imlach, another old-school die-hard against NHLPA rabble rousers.

In December 1979 the Leafs traded Sittler's good friend and linemate Lanny MacDonald, along with Joel Quenneville, to the Colorado Rockies in exchange for Wilf Paiment and Pat Hickey. Sittler immediately renounced his captaincy after reportedly ripping up his sweater. Though the animosity subsided for a brief time (Sittler even resumed being the captain) this tale was never going to end well. Sittler agreed to modify his no-trade clause and in 1982 was traded to Philadelphia for Rich Costello and a second-round draft pick.

As part of their centennial celebrations in 2016 Keon was named the greatest Maple Leaf of all-time. Sittler was listed fourth, ahead of Mats Sundin (#5) and behind Ted Kennedy (#3) and Syl Apps (#2). Famously cantankerous, Mr. Ballard was hardly one to admit an error. However, if he were alive today (he passed away in 1990) even he may agree he may have treated Mr. Keon and Mr. Sittler a little more harshly than warranted.

10

TRYING TIMES WITH THE BIG

BRASH NEIGHBOUR

What is the appropriate reaction to the brash bully-boy neighbour-nation lying across the southern border? Enthralled by American power and swagger, yet repelled by the arrogance and hubris, it is impossible for Canadians not to be preoccupied with the relationship with the United States. As Canada shifted away from British influence, were English-speaking Canadians destined to be dominated by the cultural and economic behemoth to the south? (The language divide helped maintain a more distinct Québecois culture.) In the two decades from 1960 to 1980 a definitive answer was elusive, despite Canadians spending an inordinate amount of time eagerly pointing out how they differed from Americans.

Without doubt, the relationship was, and continues to be, a complex one. Canada's only land border during the 60-80 era was with the United States. The international boundary between the two countries, including Alaska (alone having over 2,350 kilometres bordering Canada thanks to the Alaska panhandle) extends approximately 8,800 kilometres (5,500 miles) across the land, through the ocean, and between lakes. With proximity like that, coupled with American cultural, economic, and military power, the relationship was never going to be without issues.

With the advantage of hindsight, it appears that the 60–80 era provided Canada with at least a foundation for future success in developing a nascent northern vibe that was somewhat distinct from the dominant southern neighbour.

ANNOYING BEHAVIOUR FROM A POTUS OR TWO

Years before the Mulroney-Reagan lovefest of the 1980s, some Presidents of the United States (POTUS) demonstrated just how closely they valued the relationships with the leaders of their country's northern neighbour. If the belittling and bullying were indicative of how they regarded their supposed best friend, one cringes at the covert verbiage they directed at their adversaries.

Prime Minister Diefenbaker did not like President Kennedy, believing him to be arrogant and reckless. During the 1962 Missile Crisis he asked Kennedy for proof of the purported missile sites in Cuba and pushed for a United Nations team to confirm the allegations. Kennedy refused, and "advised" Canada to go to DEFCON 3 (level 1 is normal and level 5 indicates that nuclear war is imminent). The Diefenbaker Cabinet was split on the issue. Though the Prime Minister was initially opposed to Canada going on higher alert, he eventually relented.

Likewise, Kennedy was no fan of Mr. Diefenbawker, a misnomer he applied publicly to the Canadian Prime Minister not once, but twice. Kennedy even mocked Diefenbaker's French-language skills, boasting that his French, mangled though it was, was better.

The next President was Lyndon Johnson. He was a bully. He was an effective one, but a bully nonetheless. It partially explains why he was able to arm-twist members of Congress to pass such significant legislation such as the Civil Rights Act and the Voter Registration Act. He also was not shy about displaying his skills of persuasion on foreign leaders. Getting a little physical could add emphasis to the point he was making. In 1965, Prime Minister Pearson was in the U.S. and delivered an uncomplimentary speech about the Vietnam War. In a private meeting the next day a furious Johnson reportedly grabbed Pearson by the shirt, lifted him off the floor and barked, "You pissed on my rug." It can only be assumed that Pearson did not fight back—Johnson was a pretty big guy.

It is no surprise that Richard Nixon and Pierre Trudeau did not like each other. In a reversal of the cool Kennedy and the dour Diefenbaker, this time Canada had the new hip guy and the U.S. had a grouchy austere leader in President Nixon. The U.S. leader could be crude at times, as this 1971 scenario attests. On one of the infamous Nixon tapes, the President can be clearly heard referring to Prime Minster Trudeau as "an asshole." When told about the comment, Trudeau replied straight-faced, "I've been called worse things by better people."

BOMARC'S NUCLEAR FALLOUT

At the height of the Cold War with the Soviet Union Canada signed an air defence agreement with the United States. It continues to this day. Initially, Canada was eager to carry some of the military weight and the country purchased two squadrons of long-range ground-to-air missiles from the Americans. Two launch sites were constructed, one in Ontario and the other in Québec. The Bomarc missiles that were to be deployed were a less expensive alternative to the Canadian-made supersonic Avro Arrow aircraft. The fighter-jet program was cancelled, raising a howl of protest from the nascent Canadian aerospace industry. Several top-level Canadian aerospace engineers fled south to bolster the ranks of the American's National Aeronautics and Space Administration (NASA).

That the Bomarc missiles should have nuclear warheads was a no-brainer for the Americans. The Canadian government was not so sure and the Cabinet was deeply divided on the matter. Ever-wary of the increasing dominance of the Americans, a wavering Prime Minister Diefenbaker risked damaging his private parts by straddling a metaphorical picket fence as he mulled over the options. He eventually landed on the no-nuke side.

The issue was a fire-hot topic in the 1963 federal election. Lester Pearson, leader of the Liberals and a winner of the Nobel Peace Prize, argued for inclusion of nuclear warheads on the missiles. The Liberals defeated the Conservatives and Pearson formed a minority government. True to his word, Pearson allowed the missiles to go nuclear in December of 1963, a move that must have dulled the sheen on his 23-carat gold Nobel medallion.

In 1968, a new Liberal majority government under Pierre Trudeau declared that American nuclear weapons then on Canadian soil would be removed by 1972. The Bomarcs had been supplanted by newer even more effective weapons of mass destruction. The Canadian sites were dismantled and sold as scrap metal. The missiles were sent back to the United States where they were used for target practice by the U.S. Air Force.

BRIGHT DAYS FOR A BLACK ATHLETE

Johnny Bright retired from the Canadian Football league in 1964. But his saga began much before that in a U.S. college in the early 1950s. What became known as the "Johnny Bright Incident" was a racially-motivated football hit to the top-level running back in 1951—the early days of racial integration on U.S. college football teams. The incident was captured on a Pulitzer Prize winning photo sequence that was published in *Life* magazine. Bright was picked in the first round of the National Football League (NFL) draft by the Philadelphia Eagles but did not attend their camp. "I would have been their first Negro player. There was a tremendous influx of southern players into the NFL at that time and I didn't know what kind of treatment I could expect," he explained.

Bright decided to sign with the Calgary Stampeders of the Western Interprovincial Football Union (the Canadian Football League was not formed until 1958). Calgary traded Bright to Edmonton in 1954. His best years in Canadian football were with the then-named Eskimos where he helped the team win three consecutive Grey Cups in the mid-1950s. Several National Football League teams were interested in bringing Bright back to the United States. However, while playing in Edmonton Bright had started a teaching career as it was common for players of the day in Canada to have second jobs. "I'd established a home and Canada had been good to me," he said when explaining his decision to remain in the north.

When Bright retired, he was the CFL's all-time leading rusher. While the story would seem to end there, it does not. He became a Canadian citizen and eventually a school principal. In 2010 a school in the Edmonton District was named after him. The school notes that Bright was challenged by poverty and discrimination and describes him as, "A man of limitless talent, unending benevolence, and the courage of a lion."

Bright did not singlehandedly open the door for black American football players in the CFL. Nor did he shut the door on racism. The next black star running back was George Reed of the Saskatchewan Roughriders, who noted that racism's serpent head was still alive and well when he arrived in Canada the mid-1960s. However, Mr. Bright was instrumental in moving the tolerance dial forward. So too was Mr. Reed. Like Bright, he remained in Canada upon retirement and became a leader, serving two lengthy stints as the President of the CFL Players' Association—*see Chapter 9, A Country-Wide Football League.*

DOCTORS STRIKEOUT AGAINST MEDICARE

When Canadians provide examples of what makes them distinct from Americans, it is inevitable that the national health program, often labelled Medicare, is at or near the top of any list. However, what is now regarded as a national trust did not start with such overwhelming support.

By 1958 universal hospital insurance was in place across Canada as part of a joint federal-provincial funding program. In power since 1944, by 1960 the Tommy Douglas-led Cooperative Commonwealth Federation (CCF) government in Saskatchewan was ready for more publicly covered health care—much more. A bill for a universal publicly funded health program was tabled. Stormy opposition soon erupted with a barrage of hyperbole and untruths that would make some current American politicos and so-called journalists proud. Naysayers—and there were many, felt that doctors would become civil servants, unable to use their own judgement. The government could force people into certain types of care the individual did not want, or need. The costs would be prohibitive and break the treasury. People would take less care of themselves with free medical treatment. The move was only the first step toward a communist society with individual freedom abolished. These criticisms, and many more, were launched against the program.

Though Douglas left the Saskatchewan CCF in 1961 to become the federal leader of the newly formed New Democratic Party (NDP), the conflict continued to burn. On the day that the new health initiative was to start doctors in Saskatchewan went on strike. About 90 percent of the physicians participated. Only limited emergency services were available during the three-week strike that ran from July 1 to 23, 1962.

Reaction was swift. Newspaper editorials in Canada and abroad lambasted the doctors. Even the *Financial Post*, no lover of the CCF/NDP stated, "Whatever the medical politicians running the doctor strike think about the legislation, the strike they organized is an outrageous assault on organized society." The negative reaction, coupled with some eventual compromises, put an end to the actions of the picket-line physicians.

Another Saskatchewan politician, Prime Minister Diefenbaker, reacted by establishing a Royal Commission on Health Services to explore a national approach to Medicare. The Liberals, coming to power in 1963 and reliant on NDP support in the House of Commons, intensified the examination.

Like male dogs lifting their legs to urinate in the corners of suburban yards, provincial leaders fumed with righteous indignation about the federal intrusion into their domain. When the Pearson government began to open its wallet and flash a few big-denomination bills in front of their eyes, most premiers changed their tune. The federal Medical Care Act was passed in 1966 with a cost-sharing arrangement in which the federal government would pay 50 percent of the costs if the province had implemented a universal Medicare program. By 1972, all the provinces and territories were on board.

DRAFT DODGERS HEAD NORTH

Many Canadians regard the acceptance of draft dodgers from the United States as a showcase statement of their nation's separate political culture from the war-mongering Americans. It seemed to be the modern moral equivalent to those fleeing slavery via the underground railway in the mid-1800s. Before the nationalist feathers get too plumed, the 1960s Canadian support for the draft resisters was made easier by the American government providing surprisingly little pressure on Canada to alter the stance. It was almost as if the United States wanted the malcontents gone.

The welcome mat was not rolled out quickly. From 1965 to 1968 the Canadian government would not admit young Americans who could not prove that they had been discharged from military service. This resulted in a relative trickle of draft evaders entering the country.

However, that trickle quickly turned into a tsunami. In 1967 the U.S. altered the draft regulations. Male college or university students who could previously request an exemption were now eligible for the draft after completing a four-year degree, or on reaching his (only young males) 24th birthday. This had a significant impact on white, affluent young men who previously could live the life of a perpetual student and avoid the draft. By 1969 the U.S. moved to a random selection draft thus increasing the possibility that college and university students, most of them white, could be plucked from their classrooms and beer-drinking taverns and join black and working-class young men fighting in S.E. Asia. Meanwhile, at around the same time, Canadian officials ceased to ask questions about an American applicant's military service. The floodgates opened.

The Canadian government estimated that between 30,000 and 40,000 draft dodgers and about 4,000 deserters (those already inducted into the U.S. military) fled to Canada between 1965 and 1975. The group was overwhelmingly well-educated and members of middle-class families. They tended to settle in specific Canadian locations, forming a kind of ex-pat community. In an interesting twist, this draft-resister demographic and settlement pattern had similarities to the United Empire Loyalists, another politically motivated exodus from the U.S. of those who fled the American revolution. They too settled in distinct areas, largely in what is now New Brunswick and the eastern townships of Québec.

Before contemporary Canadians trumpet their country's anti-Vietnam activity, it should be remembered that Canadian companies continued to sell material that was used by the war machine. And it is estimated that the number of Canadians volunteering to fight with U.S. forces in S.E. Asia almost equalled the number of draft resisters.

With an absence of hard facts, it is difficult to gauge the number of draft resisters who remained in Canada after they were pardoned by President Carter in 1977 on his second day in office. Many estimates claim that about half of those who came to Canada stayed. In a 2001 book, Frank Kusch disputes that number, claiming that about 80 percent of the resisters eventually returned to the United States—*see Chapter 3, Night of Gastown Chaos.*

FROM CANADA WITH THANKS

"It's the most grandiose water-engineering project ever conceived for North America. It's both a monument to the ingenuity of America and a monument to the folly of the twentieth century." So said Peter Gleick of the non-profit, research-based Pacific Institute when discussing the North American Water and Power Alliance decades after the proposal.

It is not that Canada and the United States cannot cooperate when it comes to water issues. The International Commission has been operating for decades. Since the media gorges on scandal and controversy, that there is scant attention to the Commission's work is evidence that the six-person group (three Canadians, three Americans) responsible for the complex issues of cross-boundary waterways has had a long and successful history. In addition, the massive St. Lawrence Seaway project was a joint enterprise that was completed in 1959 and enabled ocean-going vessels to reach the virtual centre of the continent.

However, on occasion the Americans can get a little carried away. Some certainly did so with the idea of the North American Water and Power Alliance (NAWAPA). That the plan was initially conceived by the U.S. Army Corps of Engineers in the 1950s is a good hint that the overall benefits were going to lean toward those south of the border. That the plan became a more concrete publicized proposal in the mid-1960s, supported by several local and national politicians from the U.S. southwest, was of concern to Canadians.

Essentially, the plan called for the diversion of northern rivers (some in Alaska but most in Canada). This included the Peace, Liard, Yukon, and Fraser waterways. The diverted waters would be stored in an eight-hundred-kilometre reservoir filling the southern half of the Rocky Mountain Trench. As many as six nuclear facilities would provide power to pump water over the Rocky Mountains to Alberta, where a navigable waterway would be built to connect with the head of the Great Lakes. The rest of the water, the majority, would be funnelled to the southwest U.S. through a series of dams, reservoirs, and canals. This was no minor-league engineering project.

The estimated costs were all over the map; the equivalent of somewhere between $950 billion and $1.75 trillion in 2023 dollars. The impact of the reduced water levels of northern rivers on wildlife and vegetation did not seem to be too much of a concern for the proponents. That well over a hundred thousand people would have to be relocated; including the flooding of land that housed communities such as Golden, Invermere, Kimberley, and Cranbrook in BC, and Kalispell in Montana amongst others, did not seem to raise a great deal of alarm either. Too enamoured with the grandiosity of the scheme, the supporters did not seem to consider the likely reaction of many Canadians who may have been a tad cranky about their water being siphoned off to the benefit of the parched denizens of Utah, Nevada, and California.

Diplomatic hurdles, the rising estimated costs, and especially the increasingly vocal environmental movement railing against it put a damper on the plan. Eventually, it withered on the concept vine. However, the increasingly volatile politics in the U.S. and the long-term drought in the southwest region (despite the 2023 atmospheric rivers) could be a harbinger of things to come. As the severely overdrawn Colorado River source is being reduced to a mere trickle of what it once was, an idea with similarities to NAWAPA may be resurrected in the future.

LIGHTFOOT SONG BANNED

By 1967 Gordon Lightfoot's reputation as a folk/country/pop singer-songwriter was steadily on the rise. He was popular in Canada and beginning to be noticed in the United States. Soon he was to be more well-known south of the border.

The Black Lives Matter and related protests in the second decade of the twenty-first century had a precursor in the massive inner-city unrest in major American cities in the late 1960s. One notable example was Detroit in 1967. Ignited by a police raid on an inner-city bar, hundreds were injured, thousands arrested, and 43 killed in five days of massive race riots. Lightfoot released the song "Black Day in July" in January 1968, telling a sombre tale of the horrific event. It would not be the only time in the 60–80 era that a Canadian singer would take a lyrical shot at racism in the United States.

A few months later, Martin Luther King was assassinated by James Earl Ray. Ray fled to Toronto and acquired a Canadian passport. After a month in Canada, he travelled to England under the name Ramon Sneyd where a sharp-eyed ticket taker noticed the name on an RCMP watchlist. Ray was extradited to the U.S. He confessed and was convicted, though he later recanted his admission of guilt.

King's assassination triggered violent riots across the United States. Lightfoot's "Black Day in July," already controversial, was banned in 30 states as radio stations did not wish to "fan the flames" of racial conflict. A bitter Lightfoot said that stations wanted to, "Play songs that make people happy, not those that make people think."

Though Lightfoot's singer-songwriter career continued to rise into the early 1970s, it was not until 1974 that the single "Sundown" reached *#1 in the United States, his only song to do so.

MANHATTAN ON ICE

Several Canadians may recall the controversy surrounding the Trans-Alaska pipeline of the mid-1970s and the Exxon Valdez oil spill in 1989. The origin of the events may not be as well-stored in Canadian memory banks.

In 1968 an oil windfall was discovered in Prudhoe Bay, Alaska. Unfortunately for the oil companies it was located on the northern coast of the state which made access very challenging via the frigid Arctic Ocean. One possible method was for a super-sized icebreaker to carve a channel through the Northwest Passage so that tankers could follow, pick up the oil, and take the black gold to market. Better yet, why not design a giant oil tanker retrofitted so it could do double duty as an icebreaker? It was an interesting question. The SS Manhattan, three football fields in length with massive engines and an icebreaker bow, was the perfect answer.

A myriad of issues was raised by environmentalists—the primary one being the impact of a large oil spill in arctic waters. The Canadian government was hopping mad too. The country claimed sovereignty over the Northwest Passage, a position rejected, then and now, by the United States.

In August 1969 the Manhattan made it through the Northwest Passage. Canada made no attempt by to physically prevent the voyage. After all, there was only so much poking the American bear would take. Using a slightly revised route from the original plan, the Manhattan picked up a symbolic solitary barrel of oil and returned to base. However, a second attempt in winter failed due to heavy ice, thus revealing the potential limitations using the super tanker-cum-icebreaker model.

The sharp rise in oil prices during and after the 1973 Middle East War brought the Trans-Alaska pipeline project to the forefront. Unlike the Manhattan, a pipeline was not going to get stuck in Arctic-Ocean ice. Construction was quick (1975 to 1977), especially considering the cold weather and isolated route. The pipeline's southern terminus was at Valdez and soon the tankers were transporting the crude southward along the Alaska and BC coastline. The *Seattle Times* reported that between 1977 and 1989 tanker traffic along the west coast more than doubled. The 1989 Exxon tanker spill occurred near the Valdez harbour and spewed almost nine million imperial gallons of oil into the ocean (10.8 million U.S. gallons). The resultant environmental degradation caused new rules to be implemented that forced tanker traffic to travel much further from the coastline.

The impact of global warming reducing the ice level in the Northwest Passage means the likelihood that commercial traffic through the northern archipelago will be a hot-button issue in the future. Canada's sovereignty claims over the passage will once again likely rise to the forefront. That may be at least one reason why there appears to be more attention paid to the northern reaches of the country in the last decade or so.

OH! IT WAS ABOUT AMERICAN GIRLS!

The Guess Who's "American Woman" became the first U.S. chart topper by an all- Canadian band. With lyrics such as, "American woman, get away from me. I don't need your war machine, I don't need your ghetto scenes ... Coloured lights can hypnotize, sparkle someone else's eyes," the song was widely regarded as politically charged. The woman from the U.S. was clearly a metaphorical warning to Canadians to avoid the dark fog that so shrouded the United States at the time—primarily the Vietnam War and the race riots in major cities.

However, lyricist Burton Cummings said differently in a 2013 interview. "What was on my mind was that the girls in the 'States seemed to get older quicker than our girls and that made them, well, dangerous."

Bassist Jim Kale had a similar explanation. "We came from a very strait-laced ... laid-back country and ... there we were in Chicago, Detroit, and New York with their big-city problems. It was just a real treat to go home and see the girls we had grown up with."

Of course, the interpretation of song lyrics is the purview of the listener, despite what the songwriter says. As Paul Simon stated in "The Boxer," "All lies and jests, still a man hears what he wants to hear and disregards the rest."

Shortly after the success of "American Woman" lead guitarist Randy Bachman left the group, reportedly due to the lifestyle choices being made by his bandmates. He soon helped form the successful rock band, Bachman-Turner Overdrive which released such 1970s hits as "You Ain't Seen Nothing Yet" and "Taking Care of Business"—*see Chapter 2, Al and the Silvertones.*

PUSHING CANADIAN TALENT

It was tough being a Canadian performer in the 1960s. Radio stations ignored the supposedly second-rate home-grown talent and focussed on what was *de rigueur*—British and American music. In the TV business, it was less expensive to purchase scripted shows such as dramas and sitcoms from the United States than produce them in Canada.

A surge of Canadian nationalism spurred on by the cultural intelligentsia impacted real-life policy making in the early 1970s. Concern arose that English-language Canadian musicians could not get attention in their own country until they had an international hit. English-speaking Canadians rarely saw TV programs based in their own country except for children's shows and *Hockey Night in Canada.* Québec was the exception to the rule. Provincial government and public support for French-language music and television was consistently higher than that in the rest of the country. A vibrant localized entertainment industry was the result.

To build a dyke to hold back the American cultural flood the Canadian Radio, Television, and Telecommunications Commission (CRTC) adopted the Canadian content rule in 1971. The essence of the policy was to regulate the percentage of Canadian content to be aired. Twenty-five percent of content had to meet one of three criteria—the music or lyrics were written by a Canadian, the recording artist was a Canadian, or the record was produced in Canada, (the percentage was raised to 30 in the 1980s and 35 in 1999). Pierre Juneau was the chair of the Commission in the early 1970s and his name lives on with the Juno Awards that were established later in the decade for excellence in Canadian music

Initially, some radio stations circumvented the content rules by playing the required Canadian music in the midnight to 6:00 am time slot. These were the so-called "beaver hours." Subterfuge may even have gone as far as some Canadian TV programming being aired simply to meet the content requirements; complete with miniscule funding, terrible writing, and production values rivalling that found in junior high school shows.

Controversial then, and to a lesser extent today, Canadian content rules may be one of the few major government initiatives that accomplished what it set out to do. It provided the base to develop the more solid Canadian presence in music and television that is heard and seen today—*see Chapter 8, Two Minutes with Bob and Doug.*

SOUTHERN PUSHBACK

In the late 1950s many of the rock and roll performers were from the deep south of the United States—southerners included Bo Diddley, Elvis, Little Richard, Buddy Holly, Fats Domino, and Jerry Lee Lewis, who were heavily influenced by the blues music of that region. Then came the British invasion and being cool meant having an English accent rather than a southern drawl. Urbanized rock followed, based in San Francisco, Los Angeles, and New York.

Alas, the south had always promised to rise again. And it did. Southern rock became popular in the late 1960s and early 1970s with Creedence Clearwater Revival and the Allman Brothers Band leading the way. An anthem of sorts was "Sweet Home Alabama" by the group, Lynyrd Skynyrd in

1974. The song took a clear swipe at Canadian Neil Young who had written two well-known uncomplimentary songs about the region, "Southern Man" and "Alabama." The southern pushback song included the following lyrics:

"Well, I heard Mr. Young sing about her,
Well, I heard ol' Neil put her down,
Well, I hope Neil Young will remember,
A southern man don't need him around, anyhow,
Sweet home Alabama,"

Young responded with typical Canadian spirit, agreeing that he "richly deserved the shot Lynryd Skynryd gave me" about the song, "Alabama."

VERBAL PUNCH-UPS RE CANLIT

Growing Up Canadian is not an academic work. Not even close. However, the rapid development of Canadian Literature (Canlit) in the early 1970s to further develop a Canadian identity distinct from the Americans cannot be ignored.

In literary circles and university towers intellectual discussion and debate are a common form of conflict. If a person cannot slug an opponent on the playing field or ice surface, a good verbal punch-up in the coffee house is a suitable alternative.

One source of robust discourse for Humanities types was the distinction between literature and fiction. This difference had to be determined first before the debate could switch to an even more heated topic—Canadian Literature. While French-language writers were clearly different from those in the United States, this was not so in English-speaking Canada. There needed to be a distinct Canadian (read English-Canadian) literary voice.

The universities responded. With an increasing number of Canlit courses there had to be at least be some understanding of what the hell the subject was. Was it simply literature written by Canadians? Perhaps it was literary stories set in Canada with the author's nationality unimportant? Could genre fiction be classified as Canlit? Did the thematic thrust of the novel have to be linked in some way to the Canadian experience, whatever that was?

Important as these questions were to some students in the early 1970s, there are probably only about 200 people in the entire country who care about them today—and they work as university professors who get paid to debate such minutiae.

One constant that ran through the Canlit debates of the time was the notable contribution of women as writers and protagonists. Some novels were set in Canada, such as Margaret Laurence's trilogy about a heroine rebelling against small-town sensibilities in fictional Manawaka in Manitoba. Some were writing short stories, which opened another thrilling student debate as to whether that genre can be classified as literature. The selection committee for the Nobel Prize in Literature seemed to think so. Canadian Alice Munro began her short-story career around the early 1970s and eventually won the award, the only Canadian to do so.

Margaret Atwood, then and now, is the best known of this triumvirate that helped bring English-language Canlit to the forefront in the 60–80 era. She wrote *Edible Woman* in 1969 and described the work as "protofeminist" since it was written in 1965, years before the height of the movement. Spending an hour analyzing that descriptor would have provided a much-needed spark in an otherwise dull university seminar. Atwood became more commercially successful in the 1970s with further exploration of relationship issues in *Surfacing* (1972) and *Lady Oracle* (1976).

Female surfers were riding the new wave of Canadian literature during the late 1960s and into the 1970s. The men seemed to be stuck in the sand, watching. Their contribution would come later with the likes of Michael Ondaatje and Douglas Coupland, at a time when the previous debates about the nature of Canlit did not seem important anymore.

VIVA CUBA! VIVA FIDEL CASTRO!

So said Prime Minister Pierre Trudeau during his three-day visit to Cuba in 1976, highlighted by a much-publicized "bromance" with the bearded one. Trudeau's actions were a stark remainder that the Canadian-Cuban relationship was much more positive than that between the Americans and the island nation. It is no secret that the Canadian stance has been a craw in America's side. This was especially so in the 1970s when Canada was particularly critical of the U.S. trade embargo on Cuba. Of all the geopolitical issues in the 60–80 era, it is interesting that a small Caribbean country could be such an ongoing irritant between Canada and the United States. Perhaps Cuba was the vehicle that would prove that Canada had a foreign policy independent of the United States. Maybe Canadians simply have a hankering for quality cigars and potent rum.

Canada and Mexico were the only two countries in the Americas who did not sever ties with Cuba when Castro took power, which says much about the influence the U.S. exerted over the region in 1959. To be fair, Canada was not saddled with Cuba-oriented "complications." There were no Florida-based ex-patriot Cubans clamouring to overthrow the Castro regime and get their property back. And unlike the Americans, there were few if any Canadian companies operating in Cuba that were nationalized after the revolution. Shady Americans, not Canadians, ran the Havana casinos and dens of ill repute that were shuttered after the Batista government fell. Canada was not embarrassed by a botched invasion of Cuba at the Bay of Pigs in 1961. That sorry escapade was organized and financed by the Americans.

While the Canada-Cuba relationship has had its peaks and valleys over the years, it remains solid. Canadian negotiators and Pope Francis secretly helped broker the deal by which President Obama normalized U.S. relations with Cuba in 2014. Three years later, President Trump claimed he had cancelled the deals that had been made, though several of the agreed-upon connections remained.

WANTING SOME ARGO ACCURACY

Okay—yes, the big neighbour to the south can be annoying. But the relationship is still pretty close, so on occasion there's a need to display a little loyalty. And when that is done it is only human to hope a little recognition comes your way. Though there was an expression of appreciation at the time, once Hollywood movie-makers grabbed the story, most of the non-American aspects of what was known as "The Canadian Caper" had disappeared.

The 1979 Iranian revolution sent the Shah of Iran packing. After a few months in exile in various locales, a reluctant President Carter allowed him to enter the United States for medical treatment. That may not have been the best decision. The Shah was far from being a beacon of human rights.

Iranian militants wanted the Shah back in Iran to face whatever justice they had in mind, a fair trial being the least likely of various options. The Americans refused to ship the Shah back. That too, may not have been a good decision.

More than a bit peeved, Iranian militants seized the U.S. embassy in Teheran. The Iranian leadership seemingly supported the action. However, six American diplomats escaped. For 79 days they were harboured in the households of two Canadian diplomats, ambassador Ken Taylor and immigration officer John Sheardown. New identities with Canadian passports were developed. Two Central Intelligence Agency (CIA) operatives, one posing as an Irishman, the other a Latin American, joined the group. They posed as a film crew scouting a location for a science fiction film called *Argo*. The six "Canadian" diplomats and the two CIA operatives escaped from Iran.

The movie *Argo* was released in 2012, supposedly dramatizing what had become known to most as "The Canadian Caper." That title must have been misleading, at least to the Hollywood moguls. The Canadian contribution was given short shrift. It was as if the Canadians only played a sliver of a role despite housing the diplomats for more than two months and providing the forged documentation for the American escapees. For those who groan at the self-congratulatory tendencies of American historical movies, *Argo* was yet another example of an unfortunately long list. Despite its historical shortcomings, the movie won the Academy Award for Best Picture in February 2013.

APPENDIX A
OPENING LINES OF CANADIAN SONGS

1. "Think I'll go out to Alberta, weather's good there in the fall," (1963),
   "Four Strong Winds" – Ian and Sylvia (also recorded by Neil Young and others).

2. "He's 5 foot 2 and he's 6 feet 4, he fights with missiles and with spears," (1964), "
   Universal Soldier" – Buffy Sainte-Marie (also a hit for Donovan).

3. "When you move in right up close to me, that's when I get the chills all over me, quivers down my backbone," (1965),
   "Shakin' All Over" – The Guess Who (originally by Johnny Kidd and the Pirates).

4. "Keep your motor running, head out on the highway," (1968),
   "Born to be Wild" – Steppenwolf (one of the songs used for the movie, *Easy Rider*).

5. "When you were young, and on, your own, how did it feel, to be, alone?" (1970),
   "Only Love Can Break Your Heart" – Neil Young (reportedly written for friend Graham Nash upon his break-up with Joni Mitchell).

6. "Well, I'm on my way, to the city lights; to the pretty face that shines a light on the city nights," (1971),
   "Sweet City Woman" – The Stampeders (reached #1 in Canada and #8 in the U.S.).

7. "You get up every morning from your alarm clock's warning, take the 8:15 into the city," (1974),
   "Takin' Care of Business" – Bachman-Turner Overdrive (Randy Bachman left The Guess Who in 1970 at the height of their success).

8. "The legend lives on from the Chippewa on down, of the big lake, they called Gitche Gumee," (1976),
   "The Wreck of the Edmund Fitzgerald" – *Gordon Lightfoot* (the song reached #2 on the U.S. charts; "Sundown" was Lightfoot's only #1 U.S. hit).

9. "I cried a tear, you wiped it dry, I was confused, you cleared my mind," (1978),
   "You Needed Me" – *Anne Murray* (the only Anne Murray song to reach #1 in the U.S.).

10. "Could have been the whisky, might have been the gin, could have been the three or four six-packs, I don't know, but look at the mess I'm in," (1980),
    "Wasn't That a Party?" – *The Rovers* (as The Irish Rovers the group released the song, "The Unicorn," a major hit in 1968).

APPENDIX B

NEW HOLLYWOOD'S EMERGING STARS

1. Bonnie and Clyde (1967) – nominated for Best Picture; *featuring Warren Beatty and Faye Dunaway, with Gene Hackman and Esthelle Parsons. Parsons won the Oscar for Best Supporting Actress.*

2. The Graduate (1967) – nominated for Best Picture; *connecting Anne Bancroft with a then little-known Dustin Hoffman.*

3. Easy Rider (1969); *starring Peter Fonda and Dennis Hopper, with Jack Nicholson in a supporting role.*

4. Midnight Cowboy (1969) – won Best Picture Award; *with male leads Dustin Hoffman and Jon Voight.*

5. Love Story (1970) – nominated for Best Picture; *starring Ali MacGraw and Ryan O'Neal.*

6. Klute (1971) – a Canadian was a supporting actor; *Jane Fonda won for Best Actress and Canadian Donald Sutherland was in a supporting role.*

7. Cabaret (1972) – nominated for Best Picture; *Liza Minelli won for Best Actress and Joel Grey for Best Supporting Actor. Michael York was in a supporting role.*

8. American Graffiti (1973); *Ron Howard, Richard Dreyfuss, Cindy Williams, and Harrison Ford had major roles.*

9. One Flew Over the Cuckoo's Nest (1975) – won Best Picture Award; *Jack Nicholson won for Best Actor. Louise Fletcher won for Best Actress for her portrayal of Nurse Ratched.*

APPENDIX C

Those athletes winning the Lou Marsh Trophy as Canada's best athlete: (italics indicate those winners who are not mentioned in other Chapter 9 entries).

1960	*Anne Heggtveit*	*Skiing*
1961	*Bruce Kidd*	*Track and Field*
1962	*Don Jackson*	*Figure Skating*
1963	*Bill Crowthers*	*Track and Field*
1964	*George Hungerford*	*Rowing*
	Roger Jackson	*Rowing*
1965	*Petra Burka*	*Figure Skating*
1966	Elaine Tanner	Swimming
1967	Nancy Greene	Skiing
1968	Nancy Greene	Skiing
1969	Russ Jackson	Football
1970	Bobby Orr	Ice Hockey
1971	*Hervé Filion*	*Harness Racing*
1972	Phil Esposito	Ice Hockey
1973	Sandy Hawley	Horse Racing
1974	Ferguson Jenkins	Baseball
1975	Bobby Clarke	Ice Hockey
1976	Sandy Hawley	Horse Racing
1977	Guy Lafleur	Ice Hockey
1978	*Ken Reid*	*Skiing*
	Graham Smith	*Swimming*
1979	Sandra Post	Golfing
1980	*Terry Fox*	*Marathon of Hope*

INDEX

COMING NEXT YEAR -

Growing Up Canadian II:

CANADA AND ITS YOUTH
COME OF AGE, 1965 TO 1985.

More Humour, History, and Pop-Culture for those born in the 1950s and 1960s; including chapters on Music, Television, Fads and Fashion, Quotes, Sports, and Stage and Screen; with new features on "Tech on the Rise" and "Land and Sea."

Thanks to publishing specialist Rory Dickinson and the layout and design specialists at FriesenPress. The support was very much appreciated.

— Clyde Woolman

Printed in Canada